Building Dreams

The Homeowner's Guide to Stress-Free Home Extensions

WOODLAND PRESS

First published by Woodland Press Ltd 2024

Copyright © 2024 by Robin de Jongh

No part of this publication may be reproduced, distributed, or transmitted in any form or by any means without prior written permission from the publisher, except for brief quotations in critical reviews and certain noncommercial uses permitted by copyright law. For permission requests, contact Woodland Press Ltd.

The advice and strategies herein may not suit all situations. This book is sold with the understanding that the author and publisher are not providing legal, accounting, or other professional services. If such assistance is needed, consult a competent professional. The publisher and author are not liable for damages arising from this work. References to individuals, organizations, or websites do not constitute endorsement. Note that websites listed may have changed or no longer exist since publication.

This book seeks to provide accurate and authoritative information on the subject matter. It is sold with the understanding that the publisher does not provide professional services. The author and Woodland Press are not liable for any profit loss or other damages, including special, incidental, or consequential damages.

First edition

ISBN: 978-1-913699-08-6

*This book was professionally typeset on Reedsy.
Find out more at reedsy.com*

Contents

INTRODUCTION	v
1 DREAMING BIG: ENVISIONING YOUR SPACE	1
Defining Your Vision	1
Space Planning Basics	4
Visualising the Outcome	8
2 THE GROUNDWORK: PREPARING FOR SUCCESS	14
Budgeting Wisely	14
Choosing the Right Professionals	18
The Role of Surveyors and Engineers	21
3 GETTING THE RIGHT DRAWINGS, PLANS AND DETAILS FOR YOUR HOME...	27
The Different Kinds of Drawings	27
Which Architect or Designer to Use	31
Producing Your Own Drawings	34
Construction Specifications	37
4 FINDING YOUR IDEAL BUILDER	41
Identifying Potential Builders	41
Evaluating Builder Proposals	45
Making the Final Decision	48
5 NAVIGATING THE LEGAL LANDSCAPE	54
Understanding Planning Permission	54
Building Regulations Demystified	57
Other Legal Considerations	61
6 THE APPROVAL PROCESS SIMPLIFIED	67

Submitting Your Planning Application	67
Dealing with Objections	71
Securing Building Regulations Approval	74
7 THE TWO BUILDING CONTROL ROUTES	80
The Full Plans Route	80
The Building Notice Route	83
What to Do When Approval Fails	87
8 MANAGING THE BUILD	93
Project Management Essentials	93
On-Site Challenges	96
Keeping Up with Progress	99
9 SURVIVING WHEN YOUR HOME IS A BUILDING SITE	106
Preparing for Disruption	106
Managing Stress and Disruption	109
Keeping the Family Happy	113
10 OVERCOMING COMMON PROBLEMS	120
Budget Blowouts	120
Planning Disputes	124
Construction Issues	127
11 THE FINAL STRETCH: COMPLETION AND BEYOND	133
Approaching the Finish Line	133
Moving In	136
Transitioning Smoothly	137
Post-Project Reflection	140
SEIZE YOUR FUTURE: A CALL TO ACTION	147
About the Contributors	150
Also by Robin de Jongh	154

INTRODUCTION

Imagine transforming the space you call home into the space you've always dreamed of. A seamless expansion that not only adds value to your property but also enhances your quality of life. Whether it's creating that sun-drenched kitchen with skylights, a spacious playroom for the kids, or that tranquil home office space away from the bustle of life, extending your home can turn your current living situation into your dream dwelling.

Yet, the path to extending your home can seem fraught with obstacles, from navigating planning permissions to managing construction and dealing with the unforeseen headaches that invariably pop up. It's enough to make you think twice. But what if you had a guide that demystified the entire process, equipping you with the knowledge and tools to manage your home extension project smoothly and efficiently?

This book is designed to be that guide. It's your resource for turning daunting legal requirements and design decisions into exciting milestones. This isn't just about building extensions; it's about creating possibilities, expanding horizons, and realising visions. It's about taking that bold step towards not just enhancing your living space, but elevating your entire lifestyle.

Part One: The Vision and Its Value

Every great achievement begins with the ability to envision it. Think about the last time you felt truly at peace at home. Maybe it was a quiet afternoon with a book in a snug corner, or a lively family gathering in your dining room. Now, imagine enhancing those experiences by altering your surroundings to better fit your needs and desires. This isn't just renovation; it's transformation — not just of brick and mortar, but of life's moments.

Expanding your home is an investment in your future comfort and happiness. It's about creating a space that reflects your needs, tastes, and lifestyle. The right extension can mean more natural light flooding your interiors, more space for your growing family, better functionality with modern updates, and an increased home value should you ever decide to sell. But beyond the numbers and the aesthetics, it's about enhancing the day-to-day quality of your life in ways that matter to you and your loved ones.

Part Two: Simplifying the Complex

The thought of extending your home might bring with it a sense of dread. There are horror stories about overblown budgets, projects stretching months beyond their deadlines, and wrangles with council over planning permissions. But what if these could be navigated with a strategic approach that sets you up for success from day one?

This is where proper preparation comes into play. Knowledge

is not just power; it's peace of mind. Understanding the legal landscape, knowing what paperwork needs to be filed, what regulations need to be adhered to, and anticipating the common pitfalls can transform a chaotic experience into a structured, predictable one.

You'll learn how to communicate effectively with architects, builders, and planners. You'll discover how to set realistic timelines and budgets that keep everything on track. And you'll gain insights into selecting materials and designs that satisfy both aesthetic and regulatory requirements, ensuring that your extension not only looks good but is built to last.

Part Three: The Triumph of Creation

The real joy begins when you see your plans take shape. As walls are erected and spaces are formed, you'll witness the physical manifestation of your ideas and plans. But beyond the construction, there's the personal satisfaction in knowing you're steering the ship, making informed decisions, and watching as every element falls into place according to your vision.

And once the dust settles, what you're left with is not just more space, but a better living environment. An environment you shaped to meet your dreams. Whether it's that perfect kitchen where you'll host dinners, a special room that your children will call their haven, or simply an elegant, airy space that makes you feel more at home than ever — you will have created something enduring.

So, embark on this journey with confidence. The road to extending your home can be smooth and entirely fulfilling when you have the right knowledge and tools at your disposal. This guide is here to walk you through each phase, ensuring that every decision you make adds a brick to the foundation of your dreams.

By the end of this journey, you won't just be stepping into a larger house. You'll be stepping into a home that's a true reflection of your aspirations and a celebration of your hard work. And that's a victory worth pursuing. Let's begin the adventure of building not just an extension, but a dream.

1

DREAMING BIG: ENVISIONING YOUR SPACE

"If you can dream it, you can do it." – *Walt Disney*

Defining Your Vision

Embarking on a journey to extend your home isn't just about adding bricks and mortar; it's about realising a dream that's been brewing in your mind, perhaps for years. This initial phase, defining your vision, is crucial. It's where you translate vague ideas into a blueprint for your future space. Let's break this down into assessing your needs and desires, finding inspiration, and setting realistic goals.

Assessing Needs and Desires

Start by asking yourself why you want this extension. Is your family growing, do you need an office to work from home, or are you looking to increase your property's value? Your core reasons will anchor your project and guide your decisions.

Next, think about how this new space will serve you. If you're adding a kitchen, consider how many people you typically cook for or whether you host large gatherings. For a home office, reflect on the need for tranquillity, natural light, or storage for files and technology. It's these practical considerations that will help you not just design a space, but create a space that enhances your lifestyle.

Creating a 'wish list' can be incredibly helpful. Jot down everything you would like to include, no matter how extravagant. Later on, this list can be refined and prioritised to fit practical constraints, but initially, allow yourself to dream big. Remember, it's often easier to pare down a fantasy than to regret what you didn't consider.

Inspiration Sources

Now, let's fuel that imagination. The world is teeming with design sources to inspire you. Start with the ubiquitous platforms like Pinterest, Instagram, and design-centric sites like Houzz. They are treasure troves of visual ideas where you can create boards or save images that resonate with your aesthetic and functional desires.

However, don't just stop at digital inspiration. The real world offers a wealth of ideas. Visit homes of friends and family, home improvement shows, and even consider hotel and commercial spaces. Pay attention to how different spaces make you feel, the layouts that appeal to you, and the materials that catch your eye.

Books and magazines are not to be overlooked. There's something about flipping through pages that sparks different aspects of our imagination compared to scrolling through images online. Architectural Digest, Homebuilding and Renovating, and local home magazines can offer a plethora of ideas, often contextualised within insightful articles that might just solve a design dilemma you've been wrestling with.

Setting Realistic Goals

With a solid understanding of your needs and a head full of ideas, it's time to temper the excitement with a dose of reality. Setting realistic goals involves aligning your dreams with the practical aspects of budget, time, and space.

Firstly, consider your budget. It's easy to get carried away with all the possibilities, but it's essential to define what you can afford. Speak with professionals to get ballpark figures for the work you're considering. They can offer valuable insights into where costs typically accrue and where you might be able to save money without compromising on quality. Consider a "fabric first" approach. Don't skimp on the foundations just to get the granite kitchen island you want. It will soon get tiring when the cereal bowl starts sliding off because of subsidence!

Time is another critical factor. Understand that home extensions can be disruptive, and sometimes projects run over the estimated completion date. If you have a significant event planned, like a family gathering or a holiday, make sure your timeline accommodates these, or you might find yourself in a logistical nightmare.

Lastly, be practical about the space you have available. Every square metre counts, but there's no point in planning an extension that overwhelms your garden or changes the character of your home unless that's your intention. Local council regulations can also play a significant part in what's feasible, so make sure to do your homework on planning permissions.

In defining your vision, you're doing more than just sketching out rooms or choosing paint colours. You're crafting the framework that will guide every decision in your home extension project. By assessing your needs and desires, drawing inspiration from a myriad of sources, and setting realistic goals, you're laying the groundwork for a successful transformation of your home that truly aligns with how you want to live. This thoughtful approach ensures that the end result is not just a new space, but a space that feels like it was always meant to be.

Space Planning Basics

Understanding spatial needs

When it comes to extending your home, recognising and mapping out your spatial needs is the foundation upon which everything else rests. It's about much more than deciding where a new wall should go or what colour the curtains should be; it's about tailoring your living space to enhance your lifestyle.

Start by thinking about how you use your current space. Which areas do you find yourself gravitating towards for certain activities? Perhaps your kitchen also doubles as a meeting place for family discussions, or maybe your living room is where you exercise, work, and relax. Identifying these patterns will help you understand what works and what doesn't in your current layout.

Next, think about the changes in your life that are prompting this extension. Are you expanding your family, or perhaps picking up a new hobby that requires more space? Maybe you're working from home more and need a quiet, dedicated office space away from the household hustle and bustle. Whatever your needs, clearly defining them will make it easier to plan spaces that feel both functional and naturally integrated into your daily routine.

As you assess your needs, consider not just the quantity of space, but the quality. It's not always about adding more square metres; sometimes reconfiguring existing spaces can solve the puzzle. For instance, knocking down a rarely used internal wall could open up your space for more effective use.

Flow and functionality

Once you've mapped out what you need from your spaces, the next step is to consider the flow and functionality of these areas. Flow refers to how movement is directed through your home, while functionality is about how well the spaces serve their intended purpose.

Think of your home as a story where each room is a chapter

that should seamlessly lead to the next. Good flow between rooms can make your home feel larger and more cohesive. For example, placing the dining area close to the kitchen allows for easy serving and clearing of meals, enhancing the usability of both spaces.

Functionality, meanwhile, involves thinking about the practical details that make a space easy and enjoyable to use. This includes ample storage solutions, appropriate lighting, and the right placement of power outlets. It also means considering the ergonomics of each space. In a home office, for example, you might want windows placed to minimise glare on your computer screen, or you might need the room layout to allow for a spacious desk and easy access to frequently used files or books.

When planning for flow and functionality, don't forget to factor in your furniture and appliances. Make sure that doors and drawers can be opened without obstruction, and that there is enough walking space around furniture items. By prioritising a layout that accommodates these elements, you'll avoid common pitfalls that can make a space feel cramped and inefficient.

Future-proofing designs

Planning for the future is a crucial aspect of home extension projects. While it's important to address current needs, it's equally vital to anticipate how your requirements might evolve over time. Future-proofing your design ensures that your home remains functional and comfortable for many years to come, potentially saving you time, stress, and money on further modifications.

One way to future-proof your home is by incorporating flexible design elements that can adapt to changing circumstances. For example, a room designed for a home office might later convert into a bedroom or a hobby room. Consider using movable walls or multifunctional furniture to allow for easy reconfiguration of spaces as needed.

Another aspect of future-proofing is choosing materials and technologies that will stand the test of time in terms of durability and style. Opt for high-quality materials that require minimal maintenance and can handle wear and tear. In terms of aesthetics, while it's tempting to go with the latest trends, timeless choices often prove more prudent. Neutral colours and classic finishes are likely to appeal for longer, ensuring that your space remains stylish and up-to-date.

Lastly, think about energy efficiency. Incorporating sustainable practices and materials can significantly reduce your future utility bills and help make your home more environmentally friendly. Consider double-glazing, efficient heating systems, and renewable energy sources like solar panels. These investments not only contribute to a sustainable society but also add long-term value to your property.

By addressing these three critical aspects of space planning, you can begin to plan a home extension that not only meets your current needs but also adapts to future changes, ensuring a space that is both functional and enjoyable for years to come.

Visualising the Outcome

When you've mapped out your desires and tackled the logistics of space planning, the next exhilarating step in your home extension journey is to visualise the outcome. This process isn't just about dreaming; it's about crafting a tangible, clear vision of what your new space will look like. It's the stage where your ideas begin to take physical shape, moving from abstract concepts to sketches and models that you can see and almost touch. Here, we'll explore how sketching and modelling tools can bring your ideas to life, highlight the benefits of 3D visualisation, and discuss how to effectively communicate your vision to others.

Using Sketching and Modelling Tools

Imagine being able to see your thoughts come to life even before the first brick is laid. That's the power of modern sketching and modelling tools. Software like SketchUp is designed to be user-friendly, allowing even those without a deep background in architecture or design to build detailed, scale models of their planned extensions.

Starting with pencil sketching, you might wonder, "Why sketch if I'm no artist?" Sketching is not about artistic perfection; it's about representation and experimentation. It allows you to play with shapes, dimensions, and configurations freely. A simple pencil and paper can be enough, or you could use digital tablets that facilitate easy alterations.

Moving onto modelling, tools like SketchUp take your sketches to the next level. This software enables you to transform flat drawings into three-dimensional models. You can experiment with different materials, adjust dimensions, and even simulate lighting effects based on the time of day or the orientation of your house. These models can be incredibly detailed, giving you a very concrete sense of how your space will look and feel.

Imagine you're planning to add a large, glass-walled extension to your kitchen. With 3D modelling, not only can you determine how this will look from the outside, but you can also decide from which seat at the breakfast table you'll get the best view of your garden. You can tweak the height of the walls or the colour of the frames until everything looks just right.

Benefits of 3D Visualisation

The transition from 2D blueprints to 3D visualisations has revolutionised home planning and design. One of the key benefits is the ability to visualise the spatial dynamics of your new extensions in relation to the existing structure. You can "walk" through your home in a virtual environment, which is invaluable for understanding how the new and old spaces will interact.

3D visualisation also enhances decision-making. With a realistic model, you can better appreciate how different materials and finishes will look and feel. Will that marble countertop work better with matte or glossy cabinets? How will natural light illuminate your new living room at dusk? 3D models can help you answer these questions with greater confidence.

Moreover, these visual tools are fantastic for spotting potential issues before they become real problems. Perhaps a planned door swing cuts into an awkwardly placed column, or there's not enough room for that freestanding bath you've set your heart on. Identifying such issues early on can save you time, stress, and certainly money.

Communicating Your Vision to Others

Now, let's pivot to communication. Whether you're dealing with architects, contractors, or just trying to get your family on board with your plans, clear communication is paramount. This is where your detailed sketches and 3D models play a crucial role.

With a detailed model, you can effectively share your vision, ensuring that everyone involved understands your intentions and expectations. It helps bridge the gap between your ideas and their execution, minimising misunderstandings and discrepancies that could arise from verbal descriptions alone.

For instance, when discussing your plans with a contractor, showing them a 3D model can instantly clarify what might take hours to explain otherwise. It also allows for more accurate feedback from their end. Contractors can provide insights on structural feasibility or suggest improvements based on the model you present, ensuring that the final outcome is as close to your vision as possible.

Moreover, these visual tools can be shared with family or friends, whose support and enthusiasm for your project can be just as important. A 3D walkthrough can help them visualise the future spaces where they will make new memories, turning abstract plans into exciting, tangible realities.

In conclusion, visualising the outcome of your home extension project is not just a phase of the planning process; it's a crucial bridge between your dreams and their realisation. By harnessing the power of sketching and 3D modelling tools like SketchUp, you can explore, experiment, and communicate your vision with clarity and creativity. This not only ensures that you end up with a space that feels right but also helps in managing the practical aspects of construction and design with far fewer hitches. So, embrace these tools and step confidently towards turning your vision into a concrete reality.

RECAP AND ACTION ITEMS

Congratulations! You've just taken a significant step towards transforming your home into a space that not only meets your needs but also fulfils your dreams. By defining your vision, understanding the basics of space planning, and learning how to visualise outcomes, you're well on your way to creating a home extension that is both functional and inspiring.

Let's break down what you need to do next:

1. **Review and Refine Your Vision:** Take another look at your list of needs and desires. Have you missed anything that's essential for your lifestyle? Ensure your goals are clear and achievable. It might help to create a vision board or a Pinterest board where you can continue adding ideas and

inspirations as they come to you.

2. **Draft a Preliminary Floor Plan:** Based on your understanding of spatial needs and functionality, sketch out a rough floor plan. This doesn't have to be perfect but think about the flow of rooms and how the spaces will be used. If you're not confident in your drawing skills, simple software tools or apps can help you create this initial plan.

3. **Experiment with Tools Like SketchUp:** Now that you have a basic layout, use 3D modelling tools to bring your floor plan to life. This will help you better understand the volume of the space and the interplay of different elements. Don't worry if you're new to this – there are plenty of tutorials online that can get you up to speed quickly.

4. **Seek Feedback:** Share your 3D models and plans with family or friends. Fresh eyes can provide new perspectives and catch things you might have overlooked. If possible, consult with a professional designer or architect; their expertise can prove invaluable.

5. **Future-proof Your Design:** As you refine your plans, consider not just your current needs but also how they might change in the future. This might mean opting for adaptable designs or choosing materials and technologies that will age well both functionally and aesthetically.

6. **Set Realistic Timelines and Budgets:** Now that your vision is clearer, start thinking about the practical aspects of the project. Draft a timeline and a budget, keeping in mind that both might need to be adjusted as the project progresses.

By following these steps, you'll move confidently towards creating a home extension that not just meets, but exceeds your expectations. Remember, the key to a successful home project lies in thorough planning, continual learning, and a bit of creativity. Happy extending!

2

THE GROUNDWORK: PREPARING FOR SUCCESS

"By failing to prepare, you are preparing to fail." - Benjamin Franklin

Budgeting Wisely

Embarking on a home extension project is an exhilarating endeavour, but before you dive into the architectural sketches and paint samples, there's an essential foundation to lay — budgeting. Ensuring your finances are as well-prepared as your building plans will pave the way for a smoother, stress-free project. Let's break down the financial planning into three manageable segments: estimating costs, allocating funds, and contingency planning.

Estimating Costs

It's tempting to jump straight into the aesthetics of your extension, but first, we need to talk numbers. Estimating costs accurately is crucial to avoid unpleasant surprises down the road. Start by understanding that every project is unique, and generic online calculators can only give you a ballpark figure at best. Here's how to refine your cost estimate:

1. **Detailed Requirements**: Clarify what you want from your extension. Do you need an extra bedroom, a larger kitchen, or perhaps a sunroom? Each choice impacts your budget differently due to varying requirements for materials, labour, and time.
2. **Get Professional Estimates**: Once you have a clear idea of what you want, consult with a few architects or builders to get detailed estimates. They can provide insights into the cost implications of your specific design choices and structural needs.
3. **Include Planning and Permissions Costs**: Don't forget to factor in the costs for planning permissions, building regulations, and any other statutory approvals needed. These can vary significantly depending on local regulations and the scale of your project.
4. **Research Material Costs**: Material prices can fluctuate based on demand, availability, and economic factors. Keep an eye on these prices or discuss with your contractor who might be able to lock in prices by buying in bulk or at the right time.
5. **Consider the Unseen**: Always anticipate additional costs like site preparation, waste removal, and security mea-

sures. These might not be the first things you think of, but they can add up.

By carefully estimating these costs, you're laying a solid financial foundation that aligns your vision with reality.

Allocating Funds

With a robust estimate in hand, the next step is to allocate your funds effectively. This isn't just about ensuring you have enough money to cover each part of the project; it's about prioritising your spending to maximise the value of your extension.

1. **Main Expenditures First**: Allocate funds to the major components of the build first – structural work, roofing, and walls. These are not only crucial for the integrity and security of your extension but also represent some of the largest costs.
2. **Quality Over Cost-Cutting**: It might be tempting to go for cheaper options, but investing in quality for significant elements like windows, doors, and insulation can save you money in the long run through better energy efficiency and durability.
3. **Phased Funding**: Consider structuring your payments in phases tied to milestones. This can help manage cash flow more effectively and ensures you're not paying upfront for work that's yet to be completed.
4. **Monitor Spending**: Keep a close eye on your budget as the project progresses. Regular check-ins with your contractor can help you stay on top of any financial adjustments

needed due to unforeseen changes or challenges.

Contingency Planning

Even with the best-laid plans, unexpected issues can arise. This is where contingency planning comes into play. Having a financial cushion can be the difference between a project that stalls and one that moves forward smoothly despite hiccups.

1. **Set Aside a Contingency Fund**: A good rule of thumb is to set aside 10-20% of your total budget for unforeseen expenses. This might seem like a lot, but it can cover anything from unexpected ground conditions to changes in material prices or design alterations requested by you.
2. **Flexible Budget Items**: Identify areas in your budget where you can adjust spending if necessary. For example, you might choose a less expensive tile or forego a planned but non-essential fixture if you need to divert funds to cover unexpected structural work.
3. **Regular Reviews**: Make it a habit to review your contingency fund at each stage of the project. This will help you assess if you need to replenish it or if you can afford to redirect some of it back into other areas of your build.

By integrating these financial planning strategies into your home extension project, you are not just preparing for success; you're ensuring it. Effective budgeting is less about nickel-and-diming every decision and more about making informed, strategic choices that bring your dream home to life without the nightmare of financial strain. Remember, a well-planned budget doesn't just support your build—it ensures that your extension enhances your home and your life without breaking the bank.

Choosing the Right Professionals

Finding the right Architect or Designer

Embarking on a home extension is not just about expanding your living space; it's a journey of transforming your dreams into tangible brick and mortar. Key to this transformation is the architect or designer, who will not only draw the first line of your project but also be your guide through the labyrinth of planning permissions, aesthetic decisions, and practical functionalities.

Think of an Architect not just as a service provider but as a visionary who interprets your needs and lifestyle into spatial artistry. To find someone who fits the bill, start by asking for recommendations from friends or family who've recently undertaken similar projects. Nothing beats hearing firsthand experiences when it comes to gauging satisfaction and communication style.

Next, leverage the power of the internet. Websites like the Royal Institute of British Architects (RIBA) and the Chartered Institute of Architectural Technologists (CIAT) offer a find-an-architect service where you can browse portfolios according to your location and project type. This can be an excellent way to see who has a flair for extensions and who might resonate with your aesthetic sensibilities.

When you have a shortlist, arrange meetings to discuss your vision and see how they react. Are they listening? Do they offer creative yet practical ideas? Remember, this is also about personal chemistry. You'll be working closely with this person, so it's crucial that you feel comfortable communicating openly.

Getting the right structural engineer

While architects handle the beauty and functionality of your extension, structural engineers ensure that your dreams don't come crashing down. Literally. They are the unsung heroes who assess the viability of your plans from a buildability and structural standpoint, making sure that the new extension won't compromise your existing building.

Finding a structural engineer often works hand-in-hand with choosing your architect. Sometimes, architects have preferred engineers they work with, which can simplify communications and project coordination. However, it's still advisable to do your own due diligence.

Look for someone who is chartered with the Institution of Structural Engineers (IStructE) or the Institution of Civil Engineers (ICE). These qualifications ensure that the engineer has met stringent criteria and adheres to high standards of practice. Also look for someone who can demonstrate specific experience in home extensions.

As with architects, it's important to discuss your project in detail and gauge their understanding of your objectives. They should be able to explain complex structural issues in layman's terms.

If you leave the conversation feeling confused, it might be a sign to keep looking. After all, clear communication will be critical throughout your project, especially when unforeseen issues arise.

Vetting builders and contractors

The final piece of your professional puzzle is the builders or contractors who will bring the plans to life. The right team can mean the difference between a project that runs smoothly and one that becomes a series of frustrating or costly setbacks.

Once you have your architectural drawings, start by sourcing quotes from at least three different contractors. And while it's tempting to simply go with the lowest estimate, remember that quality and reliability are just as important. Check their references thoroughly. Contact previous clients to ask about their overall experience, timeliness, professionalism, and how they handled any issues that cropped up during the project.

Additionally, ensure that the contractors are adequately insured and check their qualifications. Are they registered with relevant trade bodies such as the Federation of Master Builders (FMB) or the National Federation of Builders (NFB)? These accreditations aren't just fancy titles; they signify adherence to industry standards and ethics.

Pay attention to how these contractors interact with you during the initial meetings. Are they punctual? Do they offer insights or raise potential issues you hadn't considered? These interactions can be very telling of their work ethic and attitude towards collaboration.

Visiting ongoing or completed projects can also provide invaluable insights into their workmanship and the durability of their constructions. After all, seeing is believing, and in the world of home extensions, the proof of professionalism is not just in the planning but in the plastering, painting, and every last paving stone.

Choosing the right professionals is more than a task; it's an investment in peace of mind. By taking the time to select the ideal architect, structural engineer, and building team, you're laying the foundation for not just a successful extension but a creation that enhances your home and life. Remember, in the realm of building and construction, every choice counts, and the right team can make the difference between a smoothly run, and a nightmare project.

The Role of Surveyors and Engineers

In the orchestrated symphony of extending your home, surveyors and engineers play indispensable roles, often unsung but crucially important. Understanding what these professionals do will help you navigate through some of the more technical aspects of your project with greater confidence.

Site Surveys

Before you so much as lay a single brick for your extension, a site survey by your architect or surveyor is usually your first port of call. Think of it as a comprehensive health check for your property and the land it sits on. It's about getting to grips with the lay of the land, quite literally. The surveyor comes in, tools in hand, and assesses the topography, existing structures, and any potential issues that might not be visible to the untrained eye.

Why should you care about this? Well, imagine you're planning to build your dream kitchen extension. You've pinned ideas, chosen your finishes, and then you find out that the ground where you plan to extend is prone to flooding, has poor soil conditions or a tangle of buried services. That's a recipe for a budget blowout or, worse, a failed project. A detailed site survey or geotechnical investigation can flag these issues before they become real headaches.

The survey itself involves a variety of techniques. Your surveyor might use laser scanning, GPS, and other tools to map out the area in detail. They'll look for boundary lines, check for any encroachments, and ensure there are no legal surprises down the line. This step isn't just bureaucratic; it's protective, ensuring that your extension doesn't encroach on protected land or breach local planning regulations.

Structural Assessments

Once the site survey confirms that your plot is viable, you'll need a structural engineer to take a closer look at what's happening beneath and around your existing structure. This is particularly crucial if you're planning an addition that will load weight onto existing walls or foundations.

A structural engineer will assess the strength and stability of your home and propose solutions to support the new structure safely. This might involve specifying the type of foundations needed, designing beams to carry extra loads, or recommending underpinning if the current foundations aren't up to the task.

For example, if you're adding a second storey, the engineer will calculate if the existing foundation can support the additional weight or if underpinning is needed. They also play a vital role in areas prone to seismic activity or mining, ensuring that the structure is compliant with safety standards that can withstand such conditions.

The engineer's drawings and calculations will be crucial when you apply for building regulations approval. Their stamp of approval assures that your extension won't collapse or cause damage to your property, allowing your property to remain saleable in the future. It's a crucial endorsement that brings peace of mind and ensures the safety and longevity of your extension.

Remember that Building Regulations are not the pinnacle of quality — they are the absolute minimum. So if you do want to future proof and exceed these minimum standards, you need to let your designers know.

Long-term Considerations

Both surveyors and engineers help you look beyond the immediate excitement of building. They "ground" your project (pardon the pun) in reality and durability. One of their key roles is to help you think long-term about your extension. This is not just about making sure it stands up today but ensuring it continues to do so in the future, regardless of what changes in your environment.

For instance, a surveyor can help you understand how planned local developments might affect your property. Is a new shopping centre going to be built nearby? This could affect traffic, privacy, and even sunlight reaching your garden. Knowing this in advance can influence design decisions, like the placement of windows or the orientation of living spaces.

Similarly, engineers help you plan for future maintenance and potential issues. They can advise on materials that are not only strong and supportive but also weather-resistant or easier to maintain. They could also design elements that make future expansions or modifications easier. This foresight can save you significant money and hassle in the long run.

By involving these professionals early in your project, you ensure that your extension is safe, compliant, and well-integrated with both your existing home and the surrounding environment. Their expertise not only helps in navigating the maze of regulations and physical challenges but also in securing the longevity and value of your home improvement investment.

Incorporating their detailed insights from the get-go isn't just about ticking regulatory boxes. It's about crafting a space that lives up to your dreams and stands the test of time – structurally, legally, and aesthetically. So, while it might seem like just another line item on your budget, investing in skilled surveyors and engineers is actually "foundational" to the success of your home extension project (again, sorry, I couldn't resist).

RECAP AND ACTION ITEMS

You've laid a solid foundation in understanding how to prepare for a successful home extension. Let's recap the essentials and gear up with some practical steps to transform your vision into reality.

First off, you tackled Budgeting Wisely. You know that accurately estimating costs is your key to reducing stress. It's what keeps your project from derailing. Ensure you've detailed every possible expense and then some. Next, allocate these funds sensibly, prioritising must-haves over nice-to-haves. And remember, the unexpected happens, so a contingency fund isn't just cautious; it's critical. Aim to set aside at least 10-15% of your total budget for those unforeseen costs.

Moving on, you dived into Choosing the Right Professionals. The importance of teaming up with the right architect or designer cannot be overstated; these are the visionaries who will bring your ideas to life. Make sure their style and experience align with your project needs. For the nuts and bolts – quite literally – a structural engineer will ensure everything stays standing, focusing on safety and compliance with building regulations. Finally, vetting builders and contractors rigorously will protect you from a world of stress. Check their credentials, previous work, and client testimonials to gauge reliability and quality.

Lastly, understanding The Role of Surveyors and Engineers showed you the groundwork in the literal sense. Site surveys, structural assessments, and considering long-term implications are all about ensuring your home's extension is feasible, safe, and a sound investment.

Here are your action steps:

1. **Create a Detailed Budget**: Start with a spreadsheet and categorise every potential cost. Consult with professionals for accurate estimates and remember to update this as you refine your project scope.
2. **Assemble Your Dream Team**: Start researching professionals now. Arrange meetings to discuss your project and sense their enthusiasm and commitment. Secure someone who not only shares your vision but can also realistically execute it.
3. **Schedule Preliminary Assessments**: Book a site survey and initial structural assessment. These evaluations will inform you about the viability of your planned extension and any adjustments needed before you proceed.

By taking these steps, you are not just planning an extension; you're ensuring it enhances your home and daily life. Get ready to see your dream space take shape, with the assurance that you've done the groundwork to support a smooth and successful project.

3

GETTING THE RIGHT DRAWINGS, PLANS AND DETAILS FOR YOUR HOME EXTENSION

"Architecture starts when you carefully put two bricks together. There it begins." - Ludwig Mies van der Rohe

The Different Kinds of Drawings

Embarking on a home extension project can be as thrilling as it is daunting. To ensure everything from your loft conversion to that sun-drenched conservatory materialises without a hitch, you'll need to start with a clear and detailed set of drawings. Think of these as your roadmap; without them, navigating through the legal, practical, and aesthetic maze of building an extension can turn into a real headache.

Measured Survey

First things first, the measured survey. This isn't just any drawing; it's the foundation of your project. Imagine trying to tailor a suit without taking any measurements – you wouldn't know where to start! Similarly, with building extensions, a measured survey gives you and your design team precise dimensions and an accurate depiction of your existing property.

A professional surveyor comes in to capture every inch of your space, noting down the structural elements, window placements, door openings, and even the orientation of the house. This survey forms the backbone of all future designs. It's crucial because any mistake at this stage could multiply, resulting in design flaws that are costly to rectify later on.

Why is it so vital, you ask? Well, imagine planning an extension that inadvertently encroaches on a non-negotiable boundary, or misjudging the slope of your land and ending up with drainage issues. A precise measured survey helps avoid these pitfalls, ensuring that your extension dreams don't float away with the first rain.

Planning Drawings

Moving on to planning drawings, these are your project's passport to reality. They transform the technical data from your measured survey into visual blueprints that detail what your extension will look like. This set of drawings needs to communicate your design vision clearly and effectively to your local planning authority, who will be looking at them closely.

In the UK, unless your extension is a permitted development (meaning it falls within certain size and scope criteria that don't require planning permission), you'll need to submit these plans for approval. Planning drawings show the proposed exterior of your building - they include elevations, floor plans, and how the new extension will integrate with the existing structure.

Here's where your vision comes to life, where you get to play around with aesthetics while also ensuring compliance with local planning policies. Think about how your extension will look from the street or how it will affect your neighbours. Your planning drawings should address these perspectives, balancing your desires with practicality and legal standards. Remember, securing planning permission hinges on how well these drawings articulate your plan.

Building Control Drawings

Once you've navigated the planning permission maze, it's time to dive into building control drawings. These are less about the broad strokes and more about the nitty-gritty details. Building control drawings zoom in on the construction aspects of your extension. They need to demonstrate that your project complies with the Building Regulations — a set of minimum standards designed to ensure the safety, health, and energy efficiency of buildings.

These drawings go deep into the specifics: materials, insulation, fire safety, ventilation, and structural integrity. They're technical and detailed, providing clear instructions for your builders. Think of them as a detailed recipe that your contractor follows, ensuring that the final build is not only beautiful but also up to code and safe.

For instance, your building control drawings will outline the type of insulation required for thermal efficiency, detail the load-bearing structures to ensure they can support the new extension, and specify safety features like fire doors and smoke alarms.

Integrating All Drawings

Each type of drawing serves its own purpose and feeds into the next, creating a comprehensive blueprint for your home extension. Starting with the measured survey, moving through the planning drawings, and culminating in the building control drawings, each step builds on the last.

Understanding these different types of drawings and their roles not only demystifies the process but also puts you in a better position to oversee your project. You'll be equipped to communicate effectively with your architect, builder, and the local authorities, ensuring that your extension project runs smoothly from paper to pavement.

So, as you embark on this exciting journey of extending your home, remember that these drawings are more than just paperwork. They are the blueprint of your vision, the guideposts that ensure your dream space becomes a reality, safely and beautifully.

Which Architect or Designer to Use

When you're gearing up to extend your home, choosing the right architect or designer is just as crucial as any concrete and beams will ever be. It's about finding someone who not only draws a plan but can see your vision, understand your needs, and translate those into a living, breathing space that you'll love. Let's explore the different professionals you can collaborate with: Registered Architects, Architectural Technologists, and Plan Drawers.

Registered Architect

A Registered Architect is someone who's not just dabbling in design but is officially recognised and registered with the Architects Registration Board (ARB) in the UK. These individuals have undergone rigorous education and training, typically involving seven years of academic and practical work. This path ensures that they are not only adept in design but also in technical and legislative aspects that are crucial in bringing your home extension from a blueprint to reality.

When you hire a Registered Architect, you're getting more than just someone who can draw up plans. You're tapping into a wealth of knowledge on sustainable design, ergonomics, and perhaps most importantly, the intricacies of planning and building regulations. They have a legal responsibility to ensure their designs are both viable and compliant with current laws, which is a massive boon. This means they're constantly up to speed with any changes in building regulations or planning laws, which can be incredibly beneficial in navigating the often tricky waters of permissions and approvals.

One of the standout benefits of working with a Registered Architect is their level of creativity and innovation. If you're looking for a design that is truly bespoke and tailored not just to your needs but also to the character of your existing home and its surroundings, an architect can bring that vision to life. They're trained to think outside the box and can provide unique solutions that you might not have considered.

However, expertise comes with a price tag. Architects generally charge higher fees than other types of designers, and their involvement can sometimes extend project timelines due to their meticulous nature and the bespoke elements of their designs. Additionally, if your project is straightforward or you have a very tight budget, you might find the cost hard to justify.

Architectural Technologist

Architectural Technologists are specialists in the science of architecture and building design. They are professionals who focus on the technical side of design, ensuring that your extension is not only beautiful but also structurally sound, energy-efficient, and built from suitable materials. These experts are members of the Chartered Institute of Architectural Technologists (CIAT).

Technologists are particularly skilled in turning architectural concepts into reality. They are adept at preparing highly detailed working drawings and have a deep understanding of construction processes. This makes them an excellent choice for projects where the technical demands are high, such as incorporating modern technologies or materials into your build, or navigating complex site constraints.

While perhaps not as focused on the aesthetic and creative side of design as architects, architectural technologists are invaluable for ensuring that your project is feasible and will pass all necessary building control checks. They often charge less than Registered Architects, making them a good middle-ground option if you need technical expertise without the higher design fees.

Plan Drawer

Plan Drawers, or drafting technicians, can be the practical choice for straightforward projects. If your extension is relatively simple — think adding a conservatory or a basic room extension — and you have a clear idea of what you want, a plan drawer might be all you need. These professionals are capable of producing the basic plans needed to get planning approval and can do so quickly and economically.

The primary focus of a plan drawer is on the technical drawing aspects of your project. They'll ensure that dimensions are correct and that everything aligns with building regulations. However, they might not offer much beyond this; the scope of their work is generally more limited, focusing strictly on the practical rather than the aesthetic or innovative.

Plan drawers are a cost-effective solution if your needs are straightforward or if you are working under tight budget constraints. Their work is less about vision and more about execution, making them a suitable choice when you simply need to move your project forward without any fuss. Some of them also have in depth local knowledge which can be invaluable in getting your extension through planning. Find these individuals by searching your local planning portal and seeing who keeps cropping up.

Choosing the right professional for your home extension project depends heavily on the nature of your project, your budget, and your expectations in terms of design and involvement. Whether you opt for the creativity and bespoke solutions of a Registered Architect, the technical expertise of an Architectural Technologist, or the straightforward, practical approach of a Plan Drawer, make sure they are someone who understands your vision and can turn it into reality. Remember, this is your space, and how it's designed and built will influence how you enjoy your home for years to come.

Producing Your Own Drawings

If you've ever fancied yourself as a bit of a designer or simply feel inspired to take a more hands-on approach to the extension of your home, then rolling up your sleeves and producing your own drawings might just be the adventure you're looking for. It's empowering, potentially cost-saving, and truly allows you to put a personal stamp on the final output. But where do you start? Let's break it down into manageable chunks: the software options, training options, and understanding construction specifications.

Software Options

Embarking on the DIY route for your home extension drawings involves getting to grips with the right software. This isn't about using Paint or a simple drawing tool; we're talking about sophisticated software that can produce detailed, accurate, and regulation-compliant plans.

One of the most accessible options is SketchUp. Known for its user-friendly interface, SketchUp offers a free online version that is perfect for beginners but can be quite limited for more complex designs. If you find yourself enjoying the process and wanting more features, you can always upgrade to their professional versions.

Another strong contender is AutoCAD. A favourite among professionals, AutoCAD is powerful with precision and versatility but comes with a steeper learning curve and a higher price tag. It's excellent for detailed work and has been used for decades for planning and building control drawings, making it a safe bet for official submissions.

For those looking to sink some more money into software, Revit by Autodesk would be ideal. It goes beyond drawing and allows for building information modelling (BIM), which means you can manage not only the physical but also the functional aspects of your building project. However be warned. Often the complexity of the software pushes you towards spending most of your time trying to get it to draw simple things using complex methods, when you could just as easily have used SketchUp or AutoCAD to do it in a fraction of the time. So for this reason I would not recommend it.

Choosing the right software often depends on your comfort with technology, your budget, and how deep you want to dive into the design process. Each option has its learning curve, but the investment in time can significantly pay off in the personalisation of your project.

Training Options

Now, unless you're a hidden architect prodigy, chances are you'll need some form of training to effectively use the chosen software. The good news is, there are plenty of options available, ranging from online courses to local workshops.

Online platforms like Udemy, Coursera, and LinkedIn Learning offer a variety of courses tailored to different levels of expertise and software types. These courses are often self-paced, which means you can fit them into your schedule without too much hassle. They also tend to be quite comprehensive, covering everything from basic navigation of the software to advanced design techniques. Go for a course that is specifically geared towards Architecture, such as my own SketchUp Pro course "*Mastering Home Extension Design*" at https://geni.us/drawingcourse.

If you prefer a more hands-on approach, look into workshops or short courses offered by local colleges or design schools. These can provide you with direct feedback from experienced professionals and the opportunity to ask questions and solve problems in real-time.

Remember, the key here is practice. The more you use the software, the more comfortable you will become. So, while formal training is invaluable, don't underestimate the power of just tinkering around and experimenting with different tools and features.

Construction Specifications

Understanding construction specifications is crucial if you're taking the DIY route. This isn't just about the aesthetics of your extension but ensuring it's built safely and in compliance with UK building regulations.

Specifications will detail the materials to be used, the standards to be adhered to, and the quality of the work required. They form part of the contract documents and are a critical communication tool between you, the contractor, and any other professionals involved in building your extension.

You can start by familiarising yourself with the Building Regulations applicable in the UK. These cover aspects like structural integrity, fire safety, energy efficiency, and accessibility. They ensure that the work is carried out to a standard that makes the building safe and environmentally sound.

Local councils often provide guidance notes and specifications for common project types. These can be extremely helpful in understanding what is expected and how to compile your own specifications.

For a more detailed approach, consider consulting with a professional who can help translate your design into a comprehensive set of construction specifications. While this does involve some cost, it ensures that your designs are practical, achievable, and compliant with all necessary regulations.

Producing your own drawings for a home extension is a challenging yet incredibly rewarding endeavour. With the right tools, a bit of training, and a solid understanding of construction specifications, you can take control of your home project and ensure it reflects your vision and meets all required standards. Dive into the details, enjoy the learning curve, and take pride in actively shaping your living space.

RECAP AND ACTION ITEMS

You've just navigated through the intricate world of drawings and plans crucial for your home extension project. Whether you're deciphering between a measured survey, planning drawings, or building control drawings, understanding these elements is foundational to achieving your dream home without a hitch.

Firstly, knowing the types of drawings required is a game changer. Each serves a unique purpose: measured surveys lay the groundwork; planning drawings help in getting that crucial local council approval; and building control drawings ensure your project adheres to all building regulations, keeping everything up to code and ensuring safety.

Next, selecting who will craft these drawings is critical. You have options: Registered Architects bring expertise and a flair for creative solutions; Architectural Technologists, with their technical prowess, ensure your plans are feasible; and Plan Drawers offer a more straightforward, often more economical approach. Choose based on your specific needs, complexity of the project, and budget.

Finally, if you're feeling adventurous and inclined to DIY, consider producing your own drawings. With myriad software and training resources available, this can be a rewarding route. However, ensure you're up for the challenge and understand the construction specifications thoroughly to avoid costly revisions. If you go this route, it may be wise to consider my online course which is specifically geared towards extension drawings (geni.us/drawingcourse).

Action Steps:

1. **Assess Your Needs**: Reflect on the scale and complexity of your extension. This will guide you in choosing between a Registered Architect, Architectural Technologist/Designer, or a Plan Drawer.
2. **Research and Select Software**: If opting to DIY, invest time in selecting the right software. Look for options that are user-friendly and specifically catered to home design.
3. **Engage with Professionals**: Even if you decide to create your own drawings, consider consulting a professional at least once. This could be a one-off consultation to ensure everything is on track.
4. **Understand Regulations**: Make sure you are up to date with local council requirements and building regulations.

This knowledge is crucial whether you are hiring a professional or doing it yourself.
5. **Plan Approval**: Before proceeding with actual construction, get your plans approved by the necessary authorities to avoid legal headaches down the line.

Remember, meticulous planning and understanding your legal obligations are the bedrocks of a stress-free home extension. Equip yourself with the right tools and knowledge, and you're set to transform your home beautifully and efficiently.

4

FINDING YOUR IDEAL BUILDER

"The bitterness of poor quality remains long after the sweetness of low price is forgotten." - Benjamin Franklin

Identifying Potential Builders

Embarking on a home extension project can be as thrilling as it is nerve-wracking. The cornerstone of a stress-free build is, without a doubt, selecting the right builder. This journey, though peppered with technicalities, can be navigated with some savvy planning and acute judgement. Let's delve into the initial stride: identifying potential builders.

Recommendations and Referrals

The most reassuring step in your builder-hunt is undoubtedly gathering recommendations and referrals. There's a special kind of comfort that comes from hiring a builder who has already turned a friend or family member's dream into reality.

So, start by tapping into your personal network. Chat with friends, family, and colleagues who've embarked on similar projects. Their firsthand experiences — the good, the bad, and the ugly — can provide invaluable insights that no online review can match.

Don't just stop at whether they liked the end product; dig deeper. Ask about the builder's communication style, punctuality, professionalism, and ability to handle unexpected hiccups. Was the project completed on time and within budget? How did the builder handle pressure? These insights can help you gauge not just the quality of the builder's work, but also their reliability and adaptability.

If your immediate network comes up short, extend your reach to local community boards or social media groups. Often, local forums and Facebook groups are goldmines of information and community feedback. Remember, the goal here is to compile a list of builders who come highly recommended for their skill and reliability.

Research and Background Checks

Once you've got a list of potential builders, it's time to switch gears to researcher mode. A thorough background check is your next best step. Start with the basics: ensure each builder is licensed and insured. This is non-negotiable. A reputable builder will have no issue providing you with their credentials, and in the UK, you can often verify these through online databases and industry associations, such as the Federation of Master Builders (FMB).

Next, delve into their portfolio. A builder's past projects are a window into their capability and style. Most established builders will have a website or online profiles where you can assess their work. Look for projects similar to yours in scale and style. This not only gives you a taste of what to expect but also demonstrates their experience in managing projects like yours.

While you're at it, don't skip the reviews and testimonials. Sites like Trustpilot, Google Reviews, and even niche construction review platforms can offer more unfiltered insights into other homeowners' experiences with the builder. Pay attention to how builders respond to both positive and negative reviews; it's a great indicator of their customer service ethos.

Finally, consider their current commitments. An excellent builder in high demand might not be able to start your project immediately, but understanding their availability will help you align your timelines realistically. It's better to get Mr right, rather than Mr right-now.

Initial Contact and Communication

With your research in hand, it's time to initiate contact. Draft a clear, concise brief of your project to share with your shortlisted builders. This should include basic details of the proposed extension, your expected timeline, and any specific requirements or challenges associated with the project. Watching how each builder responds to this brief can be very telling.

When you reach out, pay attention to how they handle communication from the get-go. Are they prompt and professional in their response? Do they ask insightful questions that show their interest and understanding of the project? Are they willing to schedule an initial meeting or site visit to discuss further?

This initial interaction is a litmus test for future communication. Remember, building an extension isn't a one-off transaction but a months-long collaboration. You need someone who is not just skilled but also communicative and responsive.

Arrange face-to-face meetings with the builders who impress you most. This gives you the opportunity to discuss your vision in detail and get a sense of their personality and working style. It's essential that you feel comfortable with them, as a good rapport will ease the process significantly.

Throughout these meetings, observe their professionalism, attention to detail, and enthusiasm for your project. They should be willing to listen to your ideas and contribute their expertise without overriding your preferences.

By the end of these stages, you should have a clearer picture of which builders are most suited to bring your dream extension to life. Each of these steps — gathering recommendations, conducting thorough research, and engaging in detailed communication — plays a crucial role in ensuring you embark on your building journey with the right team by your side.

Evaluating Builder Proposals

Once you've identified a handful of potential builders through diligent research and networking, you'll find yourself at the next critical stage: evaluating their proposals. This is where you need to switch gears from detective to analyst. The proposals you receive are more than just papers filled with figures; they are blueprints of your potential project's success or failure. Let's break this down into three manageable parts: obtaining comprehensive quotations, comparing proposals, and doing due diligence.

Obtaining Comprehensive Quotations

A quotation is not just a number—it's a builder's promise, a snapshot of their understanding of your project, and a reflection of their professionalism. To ensure you get comprehensive quotations, here's what to focus on:

1. **Scope of Work**: The quotation should clearly outline what is included in the project and, equally important, what isn't. Are there allowances for unforeseen work? How detailed is the description of the work? The more detailed, the better, as this minimises misunderstandings down the line.
2. **Materials and Brands**: You need to know what materials the builder plans to use and the quality of these materials. If your proposal includes generic terms like "standard quality", ask for specific brands or products. Remember, the durability and finish of your extension depend on the quality of materials used.

3. **Timelines**: Look for a timeline that lists not only a completion date but also key milestones along the way. This schedule should be realistic. If it seems overly optimistic, it might be a red flag that the builder is over-promising.
4. **Cost Breakdown**: A good quotation will break down costs in a way that you can understand where every penny is going. It should include labour, materials, and other charges like permits and professional fees. Watch out for large sums allocated to 'miscellaneous' or 'contingency'—these can be a backdoor to overcharging.
5. **Payment Schedule**: How and when you pay for the work is crucial. Progressive payments tied to completed stages of the work are standard. Be wary of builders who request a large portion of the fee upfront.
6. **Warranties and Guarantees**: What guarantees does the builder offer on their work? These are crucial for protecting your investment and should be included in the quote.

Once you have all this information, you'll be better equipped to compare proposals accurately.

How to Compare Proposals

Comparing builder proposals can feel like comparing apples to oranges, especially if the builders have presented their information differently. Here's how you can level the playing field:

1. **Standardise the Format**: Create a spreadsheet where you can input data from each proposal based on key factors like total cost, start and completion dates, materials used,

labour costs, etc. This visual comparison will help you spot discrepancies and outliers easily.
2. **Review the Scope of Work**: Ensure each builder has quoted for the same scope of work. If one proposal is significantly cheaper, check if they might have omitted some elements that others included.
3. **Experience and Past Work**: Consider the experience of each builder in relation to the type of work you're commissioning. Sometimes, paying a bit more for a builder with a specific expertise can save you money in the long run through better quality work and fewer errors.
4. **Soft Factors**: These include the builder's communication style, their punctuality in delivering the proposal, and the clarity of their documents. These elements can indicate their professionalism and the level of service you can expect during the project.

Doing Due Diligence

Finally, before you make your decision, you need to perform due diligence on your top choices. This is your last line of defence against potential future problems.

1. **References and Reviews**: Contact former clients to hear about their experiences. If possible, visit a current site managed by the builder to assess their professionalism and the quality of their work.
2. **Licences and Insurances**: Ensure the builder has the necessary licences to operate in your area and that they have adequate insurance, including public liability and workers' compensation.

3. **Financial Health**: If possible, get a sense of the builder's financial stability. A company facing financial difficulties may cut corners or, in the worst case, not complete your project.
4. **Legal Check**: Have a solicitor review the contract terms. Pay special attention to clauses related to dispute resolution, cancellation rights, and any clauses that seem unusual or unfair.

By methodically working through these steps, you equip yourself with a thorough understanding of what each builder can offer you. Remember, the cheapest quote might not always be the best. Value for money, reliability, quality of workmanship, and peace of mind are paramount considerations when choosing the right builder for your home extension.

Making the Final Decision

Trust and Relationship Building

When it comes to finalising which builder will turn your house into the home of your dreams, trust is not just a nice-to-have, it's essential. You're not just hiring a service; you're entering into a partnership that will affect your daily living environment for the foreseeable future. Building this trust, and ensuring there's a strong relationship foundation, is pivotal before you sign on the dotted line.

Firstly, consider your interactions up to this point. Has the builder been transparent with information and processes? Have they been consistent in their communication? Reflect on whether they have been punctual and respectful during meetings. These behaviours are indicators of their professionalism and how they value their work and clients.

Moreover, it's worth noting how they handle questions or concerns. A builder who listens to your needs and provides thoughtful, clear answers is someone who is likely aiming for a client-focused relationship rather than just a transactional interaction. They should make you feel comfortable about approaching them with any issues or questions you might have during the building process.

Another significant aspect is getting feedback from past clients. If possible, arrange to visit some of the homes they have built or extended. This not only gives you a tangible sense of their craftsmanship but also an opportunity to ask homeowners about their post-completion service. How has the builder handled any issues since finishing the project? The willingness of a builder to rectify problems and ensure customer satisfaction after payment has cleared speaks volumes about their commitment to relationship building.

Contract Negotiation

Once you've established a trust base and decided to proceed with a builder, the next step is contract negotiation. This phase is crucial as it legally binds you and the builder to the agreed-upon project scope, terms, and conditions. It's your safeguard against any miscommunications or discrepancies that might arise during the construction process.

The contract should clearly outline every detail of the project, from timelines and payment schedules to materials used and who will be responsible for what. Ensure that it also covers what happens in the event of unforeseen circumstances, such as delays due to weather or materials shortages. It's typical in building projects for some things not to go exactly as planned, so having a well-outlined process for managing changes is essential.

Don't shy away from discussing every clause that you're unsure about. It's better to address potential misunderstandings in the negotiation phase than during the build. If there's anything that doesn't sit right with you, now is the time to talk it out. You might also want to consider having a legal expert look over the contract. This could be a solicitor who specialises in property or contract law. They can provide an extra level of scrutiny and ensure that your interests are adequately protected.

Negotiation is also the stage to confirm any warranties or guarantees. These are your insurance against defects in materials or workmanship. Make sure these are written into the contract, detailing what is covered and for how long. This not only protects you financially but also gives peace of mind.

Signing the Agreement

After thorough negotiations and when you are comfortable with every aspect of the contract, it's time to sign the agreement. This is a significant moment, as it marks the point where your project officially moves from planning to action. However, before you put pen to paper, take a moment to review everything one more time. Ensure all your concerns have been addressed and that you understand each part of the contract.

When signing, it's advisable to do so in the presence of your builder and any legal counsel you've engaged. This not only ensures that all parties clearly understand the commitments being made but also reinforces the seriousness and professional nature however this isn't a legal requirement.

Remember, signing the contract is not just about legalities; it symbolises the beginning of your partnership with your builder. It's an agreement based on mutual trust and understanding with the shared goal of creating something wonderful — your dream home extension.

By the time you sign, you should feel confident in your choice. You've done your due diligence, built a relationship based on trust, and negotiated terms that protect your interests and vision. Now, it's time to look forward to the exciting phases of seeing your home extension come to life.

In conclusion, the journey to this point has required careful consideration, but the rewards of a well-thought-out decision are manifold. As you step into this next stage, carry forward the principles of clear communication and thoroughness that have guided you thus far.

RECAP AND ACTION ITEMS

Congratulations on navigating through the essential steps of finding your ideal builder for that dream home extension! By now, you've armed yourself with the knowledge to identify potential builders through recommendations, research, and engaging initial communications. You've also taken a deep dive into evaluating their proposals, ensuring that you have comprehensive, comparable quotes and have conducted thorough due diligence.

Now, having reached the cusp of making your final decision, it's crucial to solidify trust and ensure a healthy relationship with your chosen builder. Negotiating a fair contract and confidently signing the agreement are your final steps towards turning those home extension dreams into reality.

Here's what you need to do next:

1. **Compile a Shortlist**: From your research and initial conversations, draw up a shortlist of top three builders who have impressed you the most. This focused list will make your final evaluations and decision-making more manageable.
2. **Arrange Face-to-Face Meetings**: If you haven't already, arrange in-person meetings with these top builders to discuss your project in detail. It's a great way to gauge their professionalism, passion, and commitment firsthand.
3. **Review Proposals with a Fine-Tooth Comb**: Sit down with a cup of tea and thoroughly review each builder's proposal again. Use a checklist to compare key aspects like price,

timeframes, and the scope of work. Make sure everything aligns with your expectations and requirements.
4. **Seek a Second Opinion**: Before making your final choice, it might be helpful to discuss your thoughts with a trusted friend or a professional advisor who has experience in construction or legal matters. They can offer a fresh perspective or raise important considerations you might have missed.
5. **Prepare for Negotiation**: Arm yourself with knowledge about common contract terms and industry standards. Understand what you can negotiate on and what might be non-negotiable. Remember, it's not just about the cost but also about ensuring quality and timeliness.
6. **Make Your Decision**: Trust your gut, but also trust the process you've followed. Choose the builder who not only offers a fair price but also shares your vision and demonstrates integrity and reliability.
7. **Get Everything in Writing**: When you're ready to sign the contract, ensure all agreements, including any verbal promises, are clearly documented. This will safeguard your interests throughout the building process.
8. **Celebrate**: Choosing your builder is a big milestone in your home extension project. Celebrate this significant step with your family or friends and prepare for the exciting construction phase to begin.

By following these action steps, you'll feel confident and in control, knowing that you've done everything possible to select the right builder for your project. Here's to a successful build and the home extension of your dreams!

5

NAVIGATING THE LEGAL LANDSCAPE

"The law is a compass which, in the hands of a skilled practitioner, can navigate the ship of enterprise through the perilous waters of innovation." – Lord Denning

Understanding Planning Permission

Embarking on a home extension can be as exciting as it is nerve-wracking, especially when it comes to the maze of legal requirements known as planning permissions. Understanding this complex terrain is crucial to turning your dream extension into a reality, without the unnecessary drama of legal setbacks. Let's dive into what you need to know about planning permission — from when it's required to navigating the common pitfalls.

When Planning Permission Is Needed

Think of planning permission as a formal thumbs-up from your local council for proposed building works. It ensures that your project aligns with local development plans, including the appearance of buildings, the use of land, and the impact on the general environment and neighbouring properties.

Generally, you'll need to seek planning permission if you intend to:

- Build something new
- Make a major change to your building like an extension
- Change the use of your building.

If your home is listed or located in a conservation area, the rules can be more stringent. In these cases, even minor modifications can require permission.

However, not all projects require this formal nod. Smaller additions and improvements might fall under what's called 'permitted development'. This brings us to our next point.

When Does "Permitted Development" Apply?

Permitted development rights allow you to carry out certain types of work without needing to apply for planning permission. These rights derive from a general planning permission granted by Parliament, rather than from permission granted by the local council.

Here's where it gets interesting for homeowners: under permitted development rights, you can often undertake projects like small extensions, loft conversions, and changes to the interior of your building without entangling yourself in the usual red tape. However, the extent of what's allowed can vary significantly based on the designation of your area and the specifics of your property.

Before you pick up that hammer or hire your contractor, double-check the specific permitted development allowances for your home. This can typically be done through your local planning authority's website or by consulting with a planning expert. Remember, certain areas—particularly those deemed as Areas of Outstanding Natural Beauty or conservation areas—have restricted permitted development rights to maintain their character.

Common Pitfalls

Even with a clear understanding of when planning permission is needed and the scope of permitted development, homeowners can still fall into traps. Here are a few common pitfalls to watch out for:

1. **Assuming rather than confirming**: Never assume your project falls under permitted development. Always confirm with your local planning authority. This simple step can save you from costly and time-consuming enforcement actions later on.
2. **Neglecting neighbourly courtesies**: Even if you don't legally need to consult your neighbours, it's wise to keep

them informed. Surprises can lead to disputes or objections that might complicate your planning permission process.
3. **Misinterpreting regulations**: Each local authority may interpret general guidelines slightly differently. What might be permissible in one area could be restricted in another. If you're in doubt, it's always better to seek clarification than to forge ahead with misconceptions.
4. **Skipping the expert advice**: Especially for complex projects, the guidance of an architect or a planning consultant can be invaluable. These professionals can help navigate the nuanced landscape of planning permission and increase the likelihood of your application's approval.

Understanding and navigating the nuances of planning permission doesn't have to be a headache. With a bit of research, some careful planning, and perhaps some expert advice, you can manage this step of your home extension project with confidence. Whether you're adding a sunroom, converting an attic, or creating a more ambitious extension, getting to grips with the legal landscape is your first step towards a successful transformation of your home.

Building Regulations Demystified

When it comes to home extensions or any sort of building work, you might find yourself tangled in a web of technical jargon about building regulations. But fear not! Let's break down these rules into bite-size, digestible pieces so you can stride through your project with confidence, knowing that your home not only looks great but is structurally sound and compliant too.

Compliance Essentials

First things first, let's talk about what building regulations actually are. They are standards set out by the government in the UK to ensure that any building work achieves a **minimum** level of safety, accessibility, and design quality. Think of them as a rulebook that all your building work needs to play by.

When you decide to extend your home, you must make sure your plans adhere to these regulations. This is crucial not only for the safety and wellbeing of the people who will be living in or using the building but also because non-compliance can lead to some serious legal headaches down the road (and who needs that?).

Each part of your building project will need to comply with specific aspects of the regulations, from the foundations and the materials used, right up to the roof. This includes ensuring the structural integrity of the build, safe and accessible escape routes in case of a fire, sound insulation, and even the storage of fuel and waste. Building regulations can differ across the UK, so make use of your Local Authority and ask you designer if you're in doubt.

Getting approval doesn't have to be a nightmare. You have a couple of paths you can follow. One option is to submit full plans to your local council's building control body for approval before you start work. This is a thorough process but it means you get all your ducks in a row from the start. Alternatively, you can opt for a building notice which is a bit quicker and doesn't require full detailed plans upfront. However, it does carry a risk because you won't know for sure if your work complies until after it's done, which could potentially mean having to correct work later. See Chapter 6 for more details on these two routes to Building Regulations approval.

Health and Safety Standards

Health and safety is not just an annoying buzzword; it's a critical component of building regulations. These standards are designed not just to protect you and your family but also construction workers and future occupants or visitors to your home.

First up, let's talk about fire safety, which is a major part of building regulations. This includes providing adequate means of escape, installing fire doors where necessary, and using materials that help to contain a fire and slow its spread. You also need to think about the placement of smoke alarms and ensuring that any work on gas or electrical systems is carried out by a certified professional.

Structural safety is another biggie. This part of the regulation ensures that the building won't just collapse out of the blue one day. The design and construction of your extension need to support not only its own weight but also withstand external forces like wind and snow. This means using the right materials and building techniques to ensure longevity and safety.

Ventilation is another key area covered under health and safety standards. Proper ventilation is crucial to prevent dampness and condensation, which can lead to mould growth and poor air quality. This might not sound as critical as fire safety or structural integrity, but poor air quality can seriously affect your health over time.

Energy Efficiency Requirements

Last but certainly not least, let's dive into energy efficiency, which has gained increasing attention in the building regulations. Making your home extension energy efficient is not just good for the planet but also for your pocket in the long run.

Insulation plays a huge role here. Proper insulation helps keep your home warm in the winter and cool in the summer, reducing the need for excessive heating or air conditioning. This means less energy use and lower bills. The regulations specify minimum standards for thermal performance, including requirements for walls, floors, roofs, and openings such as windows and doors.

Speaking of windows, let's talk about glazing. Energy-efficient glazing helps reduce heat loss through windows, which is one of the main areas where homes lose heat. The regulations set out minimum standards for window manufacturers to follow, ensuring that your new windows help keep the heat in and the cold out.

Then there's lighting. The regulations encourage the use of energy-efficient lighting fixtures and bulbs. This might include LED lighting or smart lighting systems that reduce energy consumption by adjusting to natural light levels or by ensuring lights are only on when they're needed.

By adhering to these regulations, not only are you complying with the law, but you are also building a home that's safer, more comfortable, and cheaper to run. It's about creating a space that looks after both the people inside it and the world around it.

Other Legal Considerations

When you're diving into home extensions, the legalities don't just stop at planning permission and building regulations. There's a trio of other legal considerations that often slip under the radar but are crucial to ensuring your project doesn't hit unexpected snags. Let's unpack these: Party Wall Agreements, Rights of Light, and Access Issues.

Party Wall Agreements

Imagine you're planning to extend your home, and this involves work that affects a wall you share with your neighbour. In this case, you'll need to get familiar with the *Party Wall etc. Act 1996*. This isn't just bureaucratic red tape; it's a vital step to maintain good relations with your neighbours and protect yourself legally.

A party wall agreement is required whenever you need to carry out work involving shared walls between adjoining properties. This could be anything from cutting into a wall to install beams and lintels, to excavating close to a neighbouring building to lay foundations.

Firstly, you need to serve a party wall notice to your affected neighbour(s). You should do this at least two months before the start of the work. The notice should clearly describe the planned work and when you intend to start. If your neighbouring property is empty, fix the notice to a clearly visible part of the premises.

Your neighbours can either agree or disagree with what's proposed. If they agree, great! It's wise to have this consent in writing. If they disagree, you'll need to appoint what's known as a party wall surveyor to prepare a Party Wall Award. This is a legal document outlining what work can be carried out, how and when it will be done, and how any damages will be rectified.

One common pitfall is underestimating the time it takes to get these agreements in place. Start early to avoid delays in your project. Also, always aim for clear, respectful communication to maintain good relationships; it's often the key to smooth party wall negotiations. If after 14 days the receiving party has done nothing, a dispute is automatically deemed to have arisen. This is because the Party Wall Act requires an explicit agreement or disagreement from the neighbour.

Your local authority should have booklets providing in-depth explanation of the process, as should the Citizen's Advice Bureau and the CITB and RICS websites.

Rights of Light

This is a particularly intriguing aspect of property law. Rights of Light can indeed be a make-or-break factor in your extension plans, especially in densely populated areas. Essentially, if your extension blocks the amount of light that reaches your neighbour's windows, and this light has been enjoyed for 20 years or more, they could have a legal right to maintain that level of illumination.

Understanding and respecting Rights of Light is crucial. Ignoring them can lead to legal challenges that might not only halt your project but also be financially draining. If in doubt, it's always worth consulting a solicitor who specialises in this area. They can conduct a Rights of Light assessment and give you a clearer picture of any potential issues.

To mitigate risks, consider tweaking your designs to reduce shadow impact, or discuss with your architect how the orientation or height of your extension could be adjusted to prevent significant light loss to your neighbours.

Access Issues

Finally, we touch upon access issues, which often crop up when the extension requires use of a neighbouring property's land or when the only access to the building site is through a shared driveway or a right of way.

First up, check your property deeds for any existing rights of way or easements. If your project impacts these in any way, you'll need to negotiate with the landowner whose property is affected. This might involve temporary agreements that allow you to use additional space during construction.

If access is via a shared route, communication, as always, is key. Keep your neighbours informed and try to accommodate their access needs. Temporary disruptions should be managed respectfully and efficiently, perhaps by scheduling work that might block access at times when it's least inconvenient for others.

Sometimes, you might need to secure formal permissions or rights to use part of a neighbour's land or adjust a boundary temporarily. Legal advice is invaluable here to navigate the agreements required and ensure all is above board and binding.

While these legal considerations might initially seem just another layer of complexity, addressing them head-on is truly a cornerstone of a stress-free building project. By tackling these issues early and with professional guidance, you ensure your dream extension doesn't turn into a nightmare of delays and rising costs.

RECAP AND ACTION ITEMS

Navigating the legal landscape of home extensions doesn't have to be a daunting journey. By now, you've gained a clearer understanding of when planning permission is needed, how to leverage permitted development rights, and the common pitfalls to avoid. You've also delved into the essential building regulations, ensuring health and safety standards are met and that your extension is as energy-efficient as possible. Furthermore, you're now familiar with other legal considerations like party wall agreements, rights of light, and dealing with access issues.

So, what's next? Here are some practical steps you can take to ensure your home extension project proceeds as smoothly as possible:

1. **Research Thoroughly:** Before you begin any work, double-check your understanding of planning permissions and building regulations specific to your area. Local councils can have varied requirements, and staying informed will help you avoid costly and time-consuming errors.
2. **Consult Professionals:** Engage with an architect or a planner early in your project. Their expertise will be invaluable not only in ensuring compliance but in creatively solving any potential issues related to rights of light or access.
3. **Communicate with Neighbours:** Early and transparent communication with your neighbours can prevent disputes over party walls or rights of light. Consider setting up a meeting to discuss your plans and address any concerns they might have.
4. **Keep Documentation:** Maintain thorough records of all communications, agreements, and approvals. This paperwork will be crucial if any legal issues arise during or after your project.
5. **Review Energy Efficiency:** Revisit the energy efficiency requirements and explore if there are any new technologies or materials that could enhance your extension's performance. This could save you money in the long run and

make your home more sustainable.
6. **Plan for Contingencies:** Always have a contingency plan for time and budget. Legal and construction processes can often uncover surprises, so being prepared will help keep your project on track.

By following these steps, you can manage the legal complexities of your home extension with confidence and ease. Remember, the goal is not just to extend your home, but to enhance your living space and ultimately, your quality of life. With careful planning and a proactive approach, you'll build not just an extension, but a dream space for you and your family.

6

THE APPROVAL PROCESS SIMPLIFIED

"By failing to prepare, you are preparing to fail." – *Benjamin Franklin*

Submitting Your Planning Application

Embarking on a home extension can transform your living space, but before those dreams take physical shape, they need to navigate the paperwork labyrinth of planning applications. Let's demystify this process together, ensuring you start your project with clarity and confidence.

Required Documents

First things first, the cornerstone of your planning application is gathering the necessary documents. This isn't just bureaucracy; it's your project's first impression, presenting your vision in black and white (and sometimes, vibrant colour). Here's what you typically need:

1. Application Forms: Start with the basics. Your local council will provide standard application forms that need to be filled out meticulously. These forms are your first hurdle and need to be tackled with precision—make sure every section is completed and that no required detail is overlooked.

2. Ownership Certificate: This is a legal declaration that you own the land or have permission from the owner to submit the application. It's a straightforward document but essential.

3. Agricultural Holdings Certificate: If your property is on agricultural land, even if you're not farming, you'll need this certificate. It confirms whether or not your land is part of an agricultural holding.

4. Fee: Yes, the unavoidable application fee. This varies by location and the scale of your project, so check with your local planning authority (LPA) for the exact figures.

5. Other Supporting Documents: Depending on the complexity and type of your project, you might need to include additional reports like flood risk assessments, heritage statements, or tree surveys.

Collecting these documents might seem daunting, but think of it as gathering your troops before a battle. Each document strengthens your position, ensuring your application can proceed without unnecessary delays.

Obtaining a Site Plan

Next up, you'll need a site plan, sometimes called a location plan. This isn't just any drawing. It's a scaled diagram that shows your proposed development in relation to its surrounding environment, including boundaries and existing buildings on the site.

You can obtain these plans from several sources:

- **Local Authority:** Some councils offer a planning map service. It's a bit like ordering takeout, except instead of pizza, you're getting a detailed map of your property
- **Licensed Data Providers:** These are companies that specialise in providing accurate, up-to-date maps that comply with your LPA's requirements. They can tailor your site plan to include all necessary details such as the direction of North and the scale, which is usually 1:1250 or 1:500.
- **Your Architect:** If you obtain planning drawings from your architect then they will usually include the site plan as standard.

When submitting your site plan, ensure it's clear and legible. It should include:

- All the buildings, roads, and footpaths on or near the land
- The development's position in relation to the property boundary
- A north point to aid orientation.

Think of this plan as the stage where your home extension will unfold. It needs to be precise, clear, and informative. A well-drawn site plan not only supports your application but also helps to avoid misunderstandings or objections from neighbours or the planning authority.

Writing a Design and Access Statement

The design and access statement is needed if your project is sufficiently large or complex, so you may not need this for a small home extension. For those larger projects, it explains what you want to do and why, and how you plan to make it accessible.

If you are asked for one, your design and access statement should include:

- **The Design:** Talk about the appearance, layout, scale, and landscaping of your project. What materials are you planning to use? How will these complement the existing structures and surroundings?
- **Access:** Describe how the new development will be accessed. Consider visibility, transport options, and inclusivity. How will people get to and from your extension? How will you ensure it's accessible to everyone, including those with disabilities?

This document is your chance to convince the planning authority that your project is thoughtful, well-integrated, and beneficial. It's not just about compliance; it's about contribution—to your home and to the community.

Writing a design and access statement is like crafting a short story where your extension is the protagonist. Your goal is to make it compelling, convincing, and clear. This statement is your advocate in the planning process, illustrating your commitment to quality and sensitivity to the environment and community.

In sum, submitting your planning application is a journey that requires attention to detail, a clear vision, and strategic planning. By meticulously preparing your required documents, obtaining a precise site plan, and crafting a thoughtful design and access statement, you're not just filling out forms—you're laying the groundwork for your dream extension to take shape seamlessly. With each step, you move closer to turning your vision into a tangible, living part of your home.

Dealing with Objections

When stepping into the world of home extensions, it's as much about building bridges with people as it is about building actual extensions. You're entering a dance of diplomacy where dealing with objections becomes part art, part science. Let's break down this process into manageable chunks: engaging with neighbours, addressing concerns, and amending plans. These steps will help you navigate through any choppy waters you might encounter along your journey.

Engaging with Neighbours

First things first, talking to your neighbours can feel daunting. But remember, early engagement often leads to easier negotiations. Before you even submit your planning application, why not pop over for a chat? A friendly conversation over a cup of tea can do wonders. Explain your plans and how you think they might affect them. This isn't just courteous; it's strategic. By initiating this dialogue early, you are setting the stage for a cooperative relationship rather than a confrontational one.

When you approach the conversation, be clear and concise about what you're planning. Bring along some basic sketches or plans; these can help visualise the changes and can often alleviate concerns that are based on misunderstandings about the scope or impact of your project. Listen attentively to any concerns they might express. Remember, these are the people you'll continue to live next to, so their goodwill is invaluable.

Sometimes, despite your best efforts, neighbours might still have reservations. If they do, thank them for their input and promise to consider their concerns seriously. This doesn't mean you have to agree with everything they say, but showing that you value their peace and privacy can go a long way towards maintaining good relations.

Addressing Concerns

Once you have a clear understanding of your neighbours' concerns, it's time to address them head-on. This is where your preparation can really pay off. If noise is a worry, could you agree to restrict noisy work to certain hours? If privacy is the issue, might there be room to adjust the design to include privacy screens, or reposition windows?

It's here that your earlier work, preparing a thorough design and access statement, becomes invaluable. This document should already include considerations on how your project impacts the surrounding area, so refer back to it and see if there are already solutions to the problems being raised. If not, this is the time to get creative. Could introducing new technology or materials solve the problem? Sometimes even minor tweaks to the plans can address major concerns.

If the objections are more significant, and you find yourself at an impasse, consider bringing in a mediator. A neutral third party can facilitate a more structured dialogue and help both sides reach a compromise. It's an added expense, but think of it as an investment in both your project and your long-term relations with those around you.

Amending Plans

After gathering all feedback and weighing it against your project's needs and goals, you may find that some amendments to your plans are necessary. This is perfectly normal and, in many cases, leads to a better overall outcome.

When amending your plans, keep both the big picture and the finer details in mind. Sometimes, small changes can have a big impact on how your extension is perceived by others. Adjustments like changing materials, colours, or even the height of your extension can dramatically alter its impact on neighbours and the local environment.

Once you've made these amendments, it's crucial to update all your documents and resubmit them to the relevant authorities. This includes your planning application, design and access statement, and any other required documents. Ensure that these changes are clearly documented and explained, highlighting how they address the concerns raised.

Finally, once you've resubmitted your plans, go back to your neighbours and show them how you've taken their feedback into account. This not only demonstrates that you value their input, but it also increases the chances that they will support your project going forward.

Navigating through objections need not derail your home extension dreams. By approaching this process with empathy, openness, and flexibility, you can turn potential stumbling blocks into stepping stones. It's all about creating a balance between achieving your dream home and maintaining harmonious relationships with those around you. So take these steps seriously, and you'll find that even objections can be transformed into opportunities for better, more community-focused outcomes.

Securing Building Regulations Approval

Once you've navigated the planning application process and smoothed over any objections, the next pivotal step in your home extension adventure is securing Building Regulations approval. This isn't just another hurdle to jump; it's a crucial phase to ensure your dream extension is safe, sound, and up to the standards required by law. Let's dive into the essentials of getting this right, from obtaining detailed drawings to managing inspections, and handling any pesky non-compliance issues that might pop up.

Obtaining Detailed Drawings and Specifications

First things first, you'll need to get your hands on detailed drawings and specific specifications that comply with the Building Regulations. This is more than just a blueprint; it's the detailed anatomy of your project, showing everything from the depths of the foundations to the type of insulation in the walls.

To start, you'll want to work with an architect or a structural engineer — professionals who breathe life into the technicalities necessary for approval. These drawings must detail every aspect of the construction process to ensure that everything is up to scratch. For instance, your drawings will need to include precise details on the structural integrity of the building, fire safety measures, energy efficiency provisions, and damp proofing, among others.

It's also crucial that these documents show how your extension will adhere to accessibility standards. This might include details on door widths, ramp access, or the use of specific materials. Remember, the devil is in the details. If your documents are missing key information, expect delays or a flat-out refusal from the building control body.

Inspections and Sign-offs

With your detailed plans submitted, the next stage involves a series of inspections. These are carried out at various stages of the construction to ensure that the work complies with the Building Regulations. Typically, you'll deal with either local authority building control or an approved inspector — both serve the same purpose but operate slightly differently.

The first inspection usually happens before any concrete is poured. This 'foundation inspection' checks that the site is prepared correctly and that the foundations laid out in your plans are being adhered to. Following this, you'll have inspections possibly at the damp proofing stage, drainage stage, and pre-plastering stage. Each of these is crucial; missing one can lead to major compliance issues later.

It's worth noting that the timing of these inspections can be critical. You need to notify your inspector at various stages of the work — failure to do so can result in having to undo work for it to be checked, which is both costly and frustrating. Keep a line of open communication with your inspector and schedule ahead where possible to ensure a smooth process. Make the inspector aware if you want to be copied in on all correspondence or want to be present when the inspections are carried out.

Finally, once all the checks are done and if everything meets the standards, you'll receive the final sign-off. This is your golden ticket; it means your project complies with the Building Regulations and is safe for occupancy. It's a moment worth celebrating — all being well, of course!

Handling Non-Compliance Issues

Despite best efforts, you might find yourself facing non-compliance issues. Perhaps an inspector has flagged that a part of the construction doesn't meet the required standards, or maybe something was overlooked in the planning phase.

Whatever the case, it's crucial to handle these issues promptly and efficiently.

First, don't panic. Non-compliance doesn't mean your project comes to a screeching halt. Typically, you'll be given the chance to rectify the problem. This might involve revisiting your plans or perhaps making physical adjustments to the build.

Communication here is key. Discuss the issue with your contractor and your inspector to understand precisely what needs to be changed and why. Often, solutions are simpler than they might initially appear, but they do require quick action to keep your project on track.

In some cases, you might feel a decision is unjust or incorrect. In this scenario, you have the right to appeal, although this should be a last resort. Appeals can be lengthy and costly, so it's usually best to try to resolve issues directly with your inspector first.

Securing Building Regulations approval might seem daunting, but with meticulous planning, open communication, and a proactive approach to compliance, it's entirely achievable. Remember, this stage is not just a bureaucratic hoop to jump through; it's a quality and safety check that ensures your home extension is built to last and safe for everyone who uses it. So, take it seriously, engage with professionals, and you'll navigate this phase just fine.

RECAP AND ACTION ITEMS

Congratulations! You've just navigated the complex terrain of home extensions, from submitting your planning application to securing building regulations approval. Let's take a moment to appreciate the ground you've covered and outline some clear action steps to cement your progress.

Firstly, you've successfully compiled and submitted all necessary documents for your planning application. This includes obtaining a site plan and crafting a well-thought-out design and access statement. These documents are not only crucial for approval but set a professional tone for your project.

Next, you've tackled potential objections head-on. By engaging with neighbours early and addressing their concerns, you've fostered a communal spirit and minimised friction. Remember, amending plans isn't a setback but a strategic move towards a more harmonious and feasible home extension.

Finally, you've ensured that your building project complies with all the relevant building regulations. Obtaining detailed drawings and specifications, coupled with proactive handling of inspections and any non-compliance issues, paves the way for a smooth final sign-off.

Action Steps:

1. **Review and Organise:** Ensure all your documentation from each phase is organised and easily accessible. This will be invaluable for reference and if any further amendments or

reviews are required.
2. **Follow Up:** After submitting your planning application, don't just wait for a response. Proactively follow up with the planning department to check on the status of your application and express your willingness to cooperate and make necessary adjustments.
3. **Keep Communication Open:** Continue to maintain open lines of communication with your neighbours and the local council. Regular updates can prevent misunderstandings and keep everyone informed of progress or changes.
4. **Regular Inspections:** Schedule regular inspections with certified professionals to ensure your extension remains in compliance throughout the construction process. This proactive approach will help you address potential issues before they become problematic.
5. **Document Changes:** Any changes required by the planning department or suggested by inspectors should be documented. Update your plans and re-submit them if necessary, ensuring all changes are clearly outlined to avoid any future confusion.

By following these steps, you'll not only streamline the approval process but also contribute to a smoother construction phase. Remember, every minute spent planning and communicating effectively saves hours of potential headaches down the line. Now, take a deep breath – you're well on your way to turning your dream home extension into reality.

7

THE TWO BUILDING CONTROL ROUTES

"Failing to plan is planning to fail." - Alan Lakein

The Full Plans Route

Embarking on a home extension can transform your living space, but let's not kid ourselves—it comes with a truckload of paperwork and processes. Among the routes you can take, the Full Plans route is your go-to if you're looking for a relatively smooth sail through the regulatory seas. This approach might seem a bit daunting at first, especially if you're diving in without a clue, but no worries! Let's break it down step by step.

What Drawings You Need

First things first, you're going to need some detailed drawings, called "Building Regulations Drawings" from your Architect. Think of these as the blueprint for your project—not just a rough sketch on a napkin. These drawings are crucial because they will need to be examined by the building control officers to make sure everything is up to snuff with the current building regulations.

So, what exactly needs to be on these drawings? You'll need detailed floor plans, sections, and elevations of the proposed extension. These should include dimensions, the type of materials you plan to use, and details like insulation and fire safety measures. It's not just about making it look good; it's about ensuring it's safe, energy-efficient, and structurally sound. You will usually need to provide structural calculations and drawings at this stage too, so make sure your have engaged your structural engineer in time.

It might sound like a lot, but don't cut corners here. It's worth hiring a professional architect or a draughtsman who knows their way around the requirements. They can turn your vision into compliant plans that won't get bounced back faster than a dodgy cheque.

The Approval Process

Once your drawings are ready, it's time to submit them to the local council's building control department. This isn't just a casual handover; you need to fill out some forms and pay a fee—because, of course, there's always a fee. The cost can vary depending on the size and complexity of your extension, so check with your local council for the exact figures.

After you've submitted everything, the clock starts ticking.

The council will review your plans to ensure they meet all the necessary building regulations. This review process usually takes about five to eight weeks, during which you might need to answer additional queries or provide extra details. Yes, it's a bit like taking an exam where the questions are asked after you've handed in your paper.

If your plans are up to scratch, you'll receive a decision notice saying your application has been approved. Congratulations! This means you can proceed with the construction according to the plans you submitted. Just make sure to stick to the approved plans, or you could end up in hot water. The plans can also be approved "with conditions", which means that the plans generally meet the requirements of the Building Regulations, but there are specific conditions that need to be met before full approval is granted.

Benefits and Downsides

Opting for the Full Plans route comes with its fair share of perks. The biggest one is peace of mind. Since your plans are checked and approved beforehand, you're less likely to face nasty surprises during construction. This can save you time and money in the long run, as any major issues with compliance are sorted out before the builders get to work.

Another benefit is that having approved plans can make it easier to communicate with contractors. You can wave your set of approved drawings and say, "This is exactly what we're building." It sets clear expectations and helps in getting accurate quotes for the work needed.

However, no route is without its bumps. The Full Plans route can be slower than other options, like the Building Notice route. You have to wait for approval before starting work, which isn't ideal if you're in a hurry. And, as mentioned earlier, there's more upfront cost involved due to the detailed nature of the plans and the fees for submission.

In summary, if you're a stickler for detail and prefer everything mapped out clearly (and compliantly) before a single brick is laid, the Full Plans route is probably your best bet. It requires a bit of patience and possibly a deeper initial investment, but it smooths out potential hiccups down the line, ensuring your extension is built just the way you envisioned it—legally and safely. Ready to get started? Grab that pencil (or rather, hire someone skilled to do so) and start planning your dream extension with confidence.

The Building Notice Route

When you're diving into the world of home extensions, the Building Notice route often comes up as a nifty shortcut. It's like choosing the express lane; it simplifies the initial processes but, like any fast track, it has its quirks. Let's unpack this to make sure you're fully clued up.

What Drawings You Need

Unlike the Full Plans route, the Building Notice route is a bit more relaxed in terms of upfront requirements. Here's the kicker: you don't need to submit detailed plans right off the bat. However, don't let that fool you into thinking you need no plans at all. You still need to provide enough information to show that your work will comply with building regulations.

Typically, a basic block plan and site plan will be necessary. These should show the location of the extension in relation to the rest of your property and its boundaries. While detailed construction drawings aren't mandatory, I'd recommend having at least a drawing of the layout and critical sections. This won't just help the building control officer understand your intentions; it will also ensure that your builder is not left building your dream extension with just a rough idea of what you want.

Keep in mind that even though detailed plans aren't required initially, you should be prepared to provide them if the building control officer requests them during the inspection stages. This flexibility can be a double-edged sword: less upfront work, but potentially more down the line if your plans are not clear or detailed enough.

The Approval Process

Navigating the approval process through the Building Notice route can feel like you're trying to bake a cake without a recipe. You've got the ingredients (your building materials) and the oven (the builder), but the exact temperature and timing (the detailed plans and specifications) aren't specified until you're halfway through baking.

Here's how it typically unfolds:

1. **Submission**: You submit your Building Notice to the local council along with the required fee. This notice tells them that you plan to start work soon, and it needs to be submitted at least 48 hours before you commence any work
2. **No Initial Checks**: Unlike the Full Plans route, there's no checking of detailed plans before you begin because, well, you haven't submitted any detailed plans. You jump straight into the construction phase. Be warned, though. You should not expect the Building Inspector to be your designer or clerk of works.
3. **Inspections**: This is where the rubber meets the road. The building control officers will conduct inspections at various stages of your project to ensure that the work complies with building regulations. These stages might include foundation laying, damp proofing, and the installation of insulation, among others. Because you haven't submitted detailed plans, these inspections are critical. The officers need to see in real-time that your work complies with standards. This means you need to maintain a flexible schedule and ensure that access is available for these inspections.
4. **Completion**: Once the work is finished and compliant with the building regulations, you will receive a completion certificate. This document is crucial, especially when you sell your home in the future, as it reassures potential buyers that the work was inspected and met the regulatory standards.

Benefits and Downsides

Opting for the Building Notice route does have its appeal, but it's not without its pitfalls.

Benefits:

- **Speed**: You can start your work sooner. There's no waiting around for plans to be checked and approved, which can be a significant advantage if you're under time pressure
- **Flexibility**: You have more leeway in adjusting your plans as the work progresses. If you're the type who likes to tweak things as you go, this can be particularly beneficial.

Downsides:

- **Risk of Non-Compliance**: Without the scrutiny of detailed plans, there's a higher risk that parts of your extension may not comply with building regulations. This can lead to costly corrections
- **Potential for More Inspections**: Inspectors might need to visit more frequently to ensure everything complies with the regulations since they didn't pre-approve any plans
- **Uncertainty**: Not having detailed plans approved means you might face more uncertainty during construction. Each inspection can feel like a mini-exam where you're not quite sure of the questions beforehand.

In essence, the Building Notice route is like taking a shortcut through a scenic but unpredictable path. It can be faster and more flexible but prepare for potential bumps along the way. Make sure you're comfortable with a bit of uncertainty and are ready to adapt as needed. This route can be a smart choice for smaller projects where changes are expected on the fly, but for more complex extensions, consider whether this is the right path for you.

What to Do When Approval Fails

So, you've hit a snag with your building control approval. It's like preparing the perfect dinner party and realising you've told everyone the wrong date. Frustrating, right? But don't worry, not all is lost. Let's walk through the steps and solutions to get your home extension project back on track.

Drawings Failure

First up, we have the all-too-common scenario where your drawings are the culprits behind the approval failure. Maybe they weren't detailed enough, or perhaps they didn't quite comply with current building regulations. It's like baking a cake without enough sugar—things just won't turn out right.

What to Do:

1. **Review Feedback:** Start by reviewing the feedback from your building control officer. They'll point out where the gaps are, which is like having a cheat sheet. Make use of it!
2. **Consult a Professional:** If your drawings were a DIY attempt, it might be time to call in the cavalry—professionals like an architect or architectural designer.

These experts are familiar with the intricacies of building regulations and will help tweak your plans

3. **Resubmit Drawings:** Once your drawings are amended, resubmit them. Ensure that every detail meets the Building Regulations requirements from the Approved Documents (find them here: https://www.planningportal.co.uk/applications/building-control-applications/building-control/approved-documents).

Pro Tip: Always keep communication open with your local building control. They're like guides in this regulatory jungle and can provide invaluable advice to prevent future hiccups.

Inspection Failure

Moving on, let's say your drawings were perfect, but during the actual building phase, something went amiss. An inspection failure can occur if the work done doesn't match the approved drawings or if it fails to meet the building codes.

What to Do:

1. **Understand the Issue:** Get a clear understanding of what exactly failed during the inspection. Was it the materials used, the way something was installed, or something else? Knowing this is half the battle
2. **Rectify the Mistakes:** Depending on the issue, you might need to redo some parts of your extension. Yes, it's a bit like having to erase a part of your drawing and sketching it anew, but it's crucial for moving forward

3. **Re-inspection:** After making the necessary corrections, a re-inspection will be necessary. Make sure everything is tip-top this time around to avoid further delays.

Pro Tip: Regularly check in on the construction process, even if you've hired a contractor. Keeping an eye on the progress and ensuring that it aligns with your approved plans can help avoid inspection failures.

Retrospective Approval

Finally, if you've gone ahead and built without the necessary approvals (a bold move!), you'll need to seek retrospective approval. It's like realising you've taken a wrong turn and needing to backtrack to get on the right path.

What to Do:

1. **Assess the Situation:** First, assess how much of your construction is unapproved. It's important to understand the scope of what needs to be addressed
2. **Seek Expert Advice:** At this stage, consulting with an architect, surveyor or structural engineer is crucial. They can offer a professional evaluation of whether your existing work can meet the standards required for approval
3. **Apply for Regularisation:** You'll need to apply for a regularisation certificate, which is a retrospective approval for previously unauthorised work. It can only be done on work carried out after November 1985, and can only be done by Local Authority officers. This involves submitting drawings of the existing work, along with any additional

details required by your local building control
4. **Make Necessary Changes:** Be prepared to make changes. Your local building control may require alterations to ensure everything is up to code.

Pro Tip: *Act sooner rather than later. The longer unapproved work goes unaddressed, the more complicated and costly it can become to rectify. It's like letting a small leak turn into a flood.*

Navigating the building control approval process can sometimes feel like a maze. But with the right approach and expert advice, you can find your way out of even the trickiest situations. Remember, every problem has a solution, and with patience and persistence, you'll get your home extension project back on course. Keep your chin up and tools ready!

RECAP AND ACTION ITEMS

Navigating the building control approval process can seem like steering through a minefield with a blindfold on. But fear not! You've just armed yourself with crucial insights into the two main pathways: the full plans route and the building notice route, as well as what to do if things don't quite go according to plan.

First off, remember that the full plans route is your go-to if you appreciate a thorough check before any concrete is poured. You'll need detailed drawings and a bit of patience, but the peace of mind from gaining approval beforehand could save you from costly backtracking. If you value foresight over speed, this is your path.

On the flip side, the building notice route suits the brave at heart who prefer diving in. It requires fewer initial drawings and lets you start quicker, but carries the risk of later adjustments if your work doesn't meet standards upon inspection. If you can handle a bit of uncertainty and possible mid-course corrections, take this route.

However, not all adventures in home extensions have fairy-tale endings. If you find yourself facing a refusal, assess whether it's due to drawings not being up to scratch or an inspection hiccup. In either case, don't panic. Consult your architect or builder to amend the issues, and if all else fails, retrospective approval might be your safety net—just be prepared for the possibility of more significant changes.

Here's what you can do next:

1. **Choose Your Path**: Decide between the full plans and the building notice route based on how much upfront certainty you want versus your tolerance for risk and adjustments along the way.
2. **Gather Your Team**: Line up a reliable architect, structural engineer and builder who understand local regulations and can efficiently navigate the approval process.
3. **Prepare the Paperwork**: Whether you go for full plans or a building notice, get your drawings ready. Ensure they are detailed and clear to avoid hitches.
4. **Stay Proactive**: Regularly communicate with your local

building control body and your building team. Staying engaged can help you swiftly address any issues that arise.
5. **Plan for Snags**: Set aside a contingency budget and timeline for unexpected adjustments or the need for retrospective approval.

By breaking down the tasks and approaching each step methodically, you'll transform what seems like an overwhelming project into manageable parts.

8

MANAGING THE BUILD

"The secret of change is to focus all of your energy not on fighting the old, but on building the new." – Socrates

Project Management Essentials

Navigating the labyrinth of home extensions can feel like being tossed into a whirlwind of decisions, deadlines, and details that all need your attention yesterday. But fret not, taking a structured approach to project management can transform this chaos into a well-oiled machine, ensuring your home extension emerges just as you envisioned—without the unnecessary stress.

Scheduling

First things first: let's talk about scheduling. This is your roadmap, your blueprint for how the project will progress from week to week. It's crucial because, without it, you're essentially navigating blind. Think of it as setting up a series of dominoes; if one falls too early or too late, the whole sequence can get messed up.

Start by breaking down the project into phases. Most extension projects have similar stages: design, pre-construction (which includes all your permissions and approvals), demolition (if necessary), construction, and finishes. Within each of these, there will be a multitude of tasks that need to be scheduled.

Use a Gantt chart, a tool that helps you visualise project timelines. You don't need fancy software for this; many online tools offer free versions that are perfect for residential projects. On your chart, each task is represented by a bar spanning the start and end dates. This visual aid not only shows what needs to be done and when, but it also highlights dependencies—tasks that can't start until others are finished.

Regular reviews of your schedule are essential. Life throws curveballs, and the world of building is no exception. Regularly checking your schedule allows you to adjust and realign tasks as needed, ensuring that a delay in one area doesn't cause a cascade of setbacks.

Budget Tracking

If scheduling is your roadmap, then budget tracking is undoubtedly your fuel gauge. Keeping a close eye on your finances ensures you don't run out of steam (read: money) before you cross the finish line.

Start with a detailed budget at the outset. This should include everything from materials and labour to contingencies—typically 10-20% of your total budget, reserved for unexpected costs (and there will be unexpected costs). Itemise your budget as much as possible. The more detailed your budget, the easier it is to track.

As you progress, keep a ledger or use a budgeting app specifically designed for construction projects. Record every expense as it occurs. This real-time tracking helps you see where you're spending your money and, importantly, how much of your contingency fund remains intact.

Be proactive about cost management. Regularly compare your actual spend against your budgeted amounts. If you notice a discrepancy, don't wait to investigate. Sometimes, a simple misunderstanding or a misplaced order can throw your budget off track. Catching these errors early can be the difference between a minor adjustment and a major financial headache.

Quality Control

Last but not least, let's talk about maintaining the quality of your build. It's all well and good to keep your project on schedule and under budget, but if the quality of workmanship falls short, all your efforts will be for naught.

Quality control starts with clear specifications. These are detailed descriptions of the work you expect, the materials to be used, and the finish quality. Make sure your contractors and suppliers are clear about your expectations right from the start.

Regular inspections are vital. Don't just assume work is being done to the required standard; go see for yourself. If possible, involve an independent inspector or a trusted advisor with construction expertise to provide unbiased opinions on the quality of the work.

Act swiftly on any issues. The longer poor quality work goes unaddressed, the more costly and complicated it becomes to rectify. Address problems as soon as they are identified, and insist on corrective measures immediately. This not only keeps your project on the path to success but also sends a clear message about your expectations for quality.

By mastering these three essentials of project management—scheduling, budget tracking, and quality control—you set a solid foundation for your home extension project. With these tools in hand, you're better equipped to steer your project through to successful completion with confidence, ensuring your dream home comes to life just the way you planned it.

On-Site Challenges

Dealing with Delays

Delays can be the bane of any construction project, but they're not always a disaster waiting to happen. They're often just a part of the dance you've got to do when extending your home. First, understanding the common causes of delays can vastly improve your approach to managing them. Weather, supply chain issues, and unexpected structural discoveries are often the culprits. So, what do you do when the skies open, or a shipment of bricks goes AWOL?

Start with a proactive stance. Regularly check weather forecasts and have a Plan B for critical tasks that could be weather-dependent. For supply issues, maintain a good relationship with suppliers and have a list of alternatives who can fill in gaps when your primary choices falter.

Communication is your chief tool here. Ensure you keep an open line with your contractor about potential delays. If a delay does occur, discuss it immediately. What's the impact? How can it be mitigated? Perhaps there's an opportunity to advance another area of the project while waiting for issues to resolve.

Ultimately, flexibility and patience are key. Delays can be frustrating, but with a cool head and a clear plan, they don't have to derail your project.

Managing Subcontractors

Subcontractors are the unsung heroes of your extension project – the bricklayers, electricians, plumbers, who transform plans into reality. Managing them effectively is crucial for keeping your project on track.

First, vet your subcontractors thoroughly. Look for those with robust track records and stellar reviews. Remember, cheapest isn't always best. You're looking for value, which is a combination of price, quality, and reliability. Once you've selected your team, clarity is your next best friend. Be clear about your expectations, deadlines, and the standards you expect.

Build a rapport with your subcontractors. They should feel comfortable coming to you with problems or when they need clarification. Regular check-ins can help keep everyone aligned. This doesn't mean micromanaging – nobody likes that – but a regular presence on site and an open-door policy can make a big difference.

Sometimes, despite your best efforts, things can go awry. A subcontractor might not meet deadlines or their work might not meet your standards. Here, firm but fair communication is essential. Address issues head-on, discuss ways to rectify the situation, and if necessary, don't be afraid to make tough decisions. If a subcontractor consistently falls short, it may be time to look for a replacement.

Site Security

Site security is often overlooked until it's too late. Yet, securing your building site is crucial, not just to prevent theft or vandalism but also to ensure safety.

Start with the basics: fencing. A robust, locked perimeter fence is your first line of defence against intruders and also keeps out curious passersby who might wander onto the site and injure themselves. Lighting is another deterrent. Well-lit areas are less appealing to thieves and also make it safer for late-hour workers.

Technology has some smart solutions to offer, too. Consider

installing motion-sensor cameras or alarm systems. These can be monitored remotely and can provide alerts if anyone enters the site out of hours.

But site security isn't just about keeping people out. It's also about keeping your workers safe. Ensure that all safety gear is used properly and that everyone on site knows the safety protocols. Regular safety briefings and clear signage can go a long way in preventing accidents.

Finally, keep a detailed inventory of all equipment and materials on site, and maintain a sign-in/sign-out system for tools and machinery. This not only reduces the risk of theft but also ensures that tools are maintained and returned in good working order, reducing the likelihood of accidents caused by faulty equipment.

By taking these steps, you not only secure your site from external threats but also create a safer, more efficient working environment for everyone involved.

Keeping Up with Progress

Regular Site Meetings

Imagine you're steering a ship through ever-shifting seas. Regular site meetings are your compass and map, ensuring you don't veer off course. As you embark on the journey of building your dream extension, these meetings are pivotal to averting miscommunication and aligning every crew member to the common goal: realising your vision.

Scheduling regular site meetings allows you to establish a rhythm and routine, which is comforting amidst the chaos of construction. Ideally, these should be held weekly, providing a consistent platform to review progress, address immediate issues, and plan for upcoming tasks. During these gatherings, you'll want to have your architect (if you have kept them on during the construction phase), main contractor, and any key subcontractors present. Each has a unique perspective on the build, and their combined insights can lead to proactive solutions rather than reactive fixes.

Use these meetings to go through the work completed in the previous week. This is your opportunity to see if the actual progress aligns with the schedule. If there are discrepancies, delve into the causes and discuss ways to get back on track. It's also a wise time to preview the coming week's work. What materials are needed? Are there any expected deliveries? Foreseeing these requirements prevents delays and helps maintain momentum.

Aside from the logistical elements, these meetings are a chance for you to reassert your vision and ensure that the finer details of your home extension are not lost in translation. It's easy for contractors to get caught up in the practicalities of construction, but as the homeowner, your aesthetic and functional preferences should guide the project.

Adjustments and Approvals

Flexibility is a superpower in the world of home extensions. Rarely does a project go exactly to plan—whether it's a wall that needs to be moved a few inches to accommodate plumbing, or a window that needs resizing due to availability issues. Being prepared to make informed adjustments is crucial.

You must understand that each adjustment might require a fresh set of approvals, particularly if it alters the structure or the intended use of the space. Familiarize yourself with the local council's regulations on home extensions. Knowing who to talk to and what paperwork is necessary can streamline this potentially cumbersome process.

When adjustments are needed, document everything. Change orders are formal documents that outline the specifics of the alteration, including the scope of work, adjusted costs, and revised timelines. These documents need your sign-off before work can proceed, ensuring that you maintain control over the project's scope and budget.

Moreover, keep a keen eye on how these changes might affect your overall timeline and budget. A minor alteration might seem inconsequential, but it could have a ripple effect, impacting related tasks or requiring additional materials. Discussions in your regular site meetings should help to anticipate and mitigate these impacts.

Communication Strategies

Clear, consistent communication is the linchpin of any successful home extension project. Think of yourself as the CEO of this venture—your ability to effectively communicate your vision, decisions, and concerns will largely determine the project's success.

Firstly, establish your preferred methods of communication. Do you prefer updates via email, or would you rather have a quick call? Setting these expectations early on helps everyone stay on the same page and can reduce misunderstandings.

Technology can be a powerful ally here. Various project management tools are available that can help you keep track of progress, deadlines, and budgets. These platforms often allow you to communicate with your team, share documents, and update task lists in real time. Apps like Trello, Asana, or even dedicated construction management software can offer you a dashboard view of your project, making it easier to keep your finger on the pulse without needing to be on-site every day. However, don't try to foist these tools on your contractors or designers, as they will have their own ways of working and won't necessarily appreciate you expecting them to use yours!

A more readily appreciated communication strategy involves being on-site regularly. While regular meetings are crucial, there's no substitute for seeing the progress with your own eyes. These visits can reveal a lot about the day-to-day operations and give you a clearer perspective on any issues that might not be fully captured in reports or emails.

During these visits, engage not only with your main contractor but also with the subcontractors. These are the individuals turning your plans into reality; building a good rapport with them can help ensure they understand your priorities and take ownership of their role in your project.

Lastly, always foster an environment where questions or concerns can be raised. Encourage your team to communicate openly and without fear of reprisal. The more comfortable they feel in sharing information, the more likely you are to catch potential issues before they become costly problems.

By integrating these strategies into your project, you not only keep your finger on the pulse but also drive your project forward with confidence and control. As you navigate through regular site meetings, adjustments and approvals, and refined communication tactics, you'll find that managing the build becomes not just about overseeing construction but steering your vision to its grand completion.

RECAP AND ACTION ITEMS

Congratulations! You've navigated through the vital aspects of managing the build for your home extension. By grasping the essentials of project management, tackling on-site challenges, and keeping up with progress, you're well-equipped to steer your project towards success.

Let's ensure all that knowledge translates into action. Here are some practical steps to implement what you've learned:

1. **Create a Master Schedule**: Using tools like Gantt charts, outline every phase of your project. Include key milestones and integrate buffer times for unexpected delays. This visual representation will help you and everyone involved stay on track.
2. **Set Up a Budget Tracker**: Whether it's a spreadsheet or a specialised software, begin tracking every expense against

your initial budget. Regularly update this to avoid any financial surprises. Remember, being proactive is cheaper than being reactive.
3. **Implement Quality Checks**: Establish weekly quality control checks. Use checklists tailored to different stages of the construction to ensure nothing is missed and everything meets your standards.
4. **Prepare for Delays**: They're almost inevitable, but don't despair. Develop a plan for potential delays, perhaps a list of immediate actions or backup subcontractors who can jump in if needed. Flexibility can be your best tool here.
5. **Manage Subcontractors Firmly and Fairly**: Keep a regular schedule for updates and meetings with your subcontractors. Clear, documented communications and agreed milestones will help keep everyone accountable and motivated.
6. **Secure Your Site**: Invest in good lighting, sturdy fences, and perhaps CCTV systems. Also, ensure your insurance covers construction-specific risks.
7. **Hold Regular Site Meetings**: These should be brief but frequent. They're crucial for catching issues early and adjusting plans smoothly without major disruptions.
8. **Adjustments and Approvals**: Keep a log of all changes, however minor they seem. This will be invaluable for both tracking progress and for final approvals from local authorities.
9. **Enhance Your Communication**: Develop a communication plan that specifies who needs what information and when. Effective communication can often be the difference between a project that flounders and one that flourishes.

By following these steps, you not only enhance your capability to manage the build effectively but also increase the likelihood of completing your home extension on time, within budget, and to your desired quality. Remember, a well-managed build is less stressful and more successful. Here's to building your dreams into reality!

9

SURVIVING WHEN YOUR HOME IS A BUILDING SITE

"Chaos often breeds life, when order breeds habit." - Henry Adams

Preparing for Disruption

Embarking on a home extension is much like setting sail into a storm. It's thrilling, sure, but without the right preparations, it's just plain reckless. Let's get you shipshape with some savvy strategies to minimize the chaos and keep your sanity intact.

Planning Ahead

The key to reducing stress during a construction project is all about foresight. Think of it as setting the stage for a performance where you and your builders are the main actors. The script? A detailed project plan.

First off, you need a clear, actionable timeline. Sit down with your contractor and discuss the phases of your extension. When will the demolition start? What about the noise peaks? Knowing the schedule will help you anticipate the most disruptive times and plan around them.

Next, budget planning is crucial—not just for the build, but for your daily living too. With parts of your home becoming a temporary war zone, there might be days when cooking is just not feasible. Set aside a realistic budget for takeaways and meals out. Also, consider the little costs that add up, like extra cups of coffee when your kitchen is a pile of rubble.

Lastly, get your paperwork in order. Ensure that all permits are secured and that you understand local regulations. Being caught off guard by legalities can delay your project and lead to unnecessary stress.

Setting Up Temporary Spaces

Your home will feel like a puzzle in disarray during the extension, but setting up effective temporary spaces can be a game-changer.

Start with living essentials. Identify which parts of your home will be affected during each phase of construction and plan accordingly. If your kitchen is getting extended, set up a mini kitchenette in another room with essentials like a microwave, a mini-fridge, and a kettle. It might not be haute cuisine, but it'll keep you fuelled.

For your makeshift living areas, think comfort and practicality. Move your favourite armchair, throw in some cosy blankets, and ensure good lighting. This will be your sanctuary, so make it feel as homely as possible. Portable wardrobes and drawers can help organise your belongings and keep the dust off your clothes.

Don't overlook your bathroom arrangements. If your main bathroom will be out of commission, consider if you'll need to set up temporary solutions or schedule access times if you have an alternative bathroom.

And what about your digital life? Ensure you have a Wi-Fi extension if needed, so your temporary spaces are as connected as the rest of your house. This is crucial if you're working from home or have teenagers in the house.

Builder's Storage

The last thing you want during a home extension is tripping over building materials and tools. Effective storage solutions will protect your peace of mind and your project materials.

First, discuss with your builder where the storage area will be located. It should be accessible but out of the way of daily activities to avoid any disruptions. If space is tight, consider hiring a temporary storage unit. These come in various sizes and can be a godsend for keeping things organised and secure.

Protect your belongings from dust and damage. Cover furniture with dust sheets and seal off rooms that are not being worked on with plastic sheeting or temporary doors. It's also wise to store valuable items like paintings, vases, and electronic devices away from the construction zone.

Lastly, safety is paramount. Ensure that the storage area is safe and secure, with all tools and materials neatly stored at the end of each day. This not only prevents accidents but also discourages any potential theft.

By thinking ahead, setting up functional temporary spaces, and organising builder's storage effectively, you'll navigate the chaos of living through a home extension. Remember, preparation is your best defence against the stresses and strains of this tumultuous time. Keep your eye on the prize—a beautifully extended home—and let these strategies guide you through the storm.

Managing Stress and Disruption

Maintaining Routine During The Building Phase

When your home turns into a construction site, everyday life can feel like navigating a maze blindfolded. However, maintaining a semblance of routine amidst the chaos is not just possible; it's essential for your sanity. Think of routine as your secret weapon in combating the stress and unpredictability of home extensions.

Start by identifying the non-negotiables in your daily schedule. Whether it's your morning coffee, a jog, or getting the kids ready for school, ensure these activities have a protected slot.

It might sound simplistic, but having these constants provides a psychological anchor, stabilising your day from the outset.

Next, consider the timing of your construction activities. Discuss with your builder or contractor to establish a daily start and finish time that respects your essential routines. If you work from home, perhaps quieter tasks could be scheduled around your major work hours, or noisy activities aligned with your time away from your desk.

Adapting your routine to fit the new temporary living situation is also crucial. For instance, if your kitchen is out of commission, a temporary setup with a microwave, toaster, and kettle in another room might become your new place to prepare simple meals. The key here is to simplify rather than replicate. Think of it as streamlining your life to suit the current circumstances, reducing decision fatigue, and keeping stress at bay.

Finally, don't forget to pencil in downtime. Construction can be all-consuming, and it's easy to spend every waking moment thinking about it. Schedule regular breaks from the chaos. Perhaps a weekly family movie night, even if it's on a laptop in the bedroom, can be a perfect escape from the dust and noise.

Open Communication and Flexibility

You've probably heard the phrase, "Communication is key," more times than you can count, but when it comes to surviving a home renovation, it couldn't be more true. Keeping an open line of communication with your builders, family, and even neighbours can significantly reduce misunderstandings and stress.

Start with regular check-ins with your contractor. These don't have to be long, drawn-out meetings; a quick 15-minute chat each morning could suffice. Use this time to discuss the day's activities, any concerns you have, and adjustments to the plan. This not only keeps you informed but also builds a rapport that can make it easier to handle any issues that might arise.

Flexibility is the companion to communication. While it's great to have a plan, the nature of building work means that unexpected issues can crop up. Whether it's a delay in materials, weather setbacks, or discovering unexpected structural issues, being prepared to adapt is crucial. This might mean shifting your temporary kitchen to another room or adjusting your schedule to accommodate quieter mornings. The more adaptable you are, the less stressful these changes will feel.

Don't overlook the importance of communicating with your family as well. Regular family meetings can help everyone stay on the same page about what's happening and voice any concerns or frustrations. This can be particularly important for children, who might feel unsettled by the upheaval. Keeping them informed can help mitigate feelings of anxiety.

Health and Safety

Living through a home extension project isn't just chaotic; it can also pose health and safety risks that you need to be acutely aware of. Prioritising safety can prevent accidents and ensure that your living environment is as healthy as possible, even in the midst of a building site.

Firstly, establish clear safety protocols with your builders. This includes agreeing on which areas of the home will be construction zones and which will be strictly off-limits to ensure the safety of your family. Make sure that these areas are clearly marked, perhaps with barriers or signs, to remind everyone, especially children, to steer clear.

Dust and debris are almost unavoidable with construction but managing them proactively can minimise health risks. Ensure that your contractor uses dust sheets and that there's adequate ventilation to prevent dust from settling throughout the house. For particularly intense phases of construction, consider arranging a temporary off-site living situation or day excursions for the family to escape the worst of it.

Noise is another stress factor that can affect your wellbeing. While some noise is inevitable, discuss with your contractor any measures they can take to minimise it, such as using quieter tools or carrying out the loudest tasks at less disruptive times. For your part, investing in noise-cancelling headphones could be a worthwhile consideration, providing a respite from the relentless clamour.

Finally, maintain a regular cleaning schedule. It might seem futile to clean when every day brings new layers of dust, but keeping on top of it can prevent the build-up from becoming unmanageable. It also contributes to creating a sense of normalcy and control amidst the disorder.

Surviving a home extension with your sanity intact requires a blend of solid planning, open communication, and a commitment to maintaining routine. By managing these elements effectively, the disruption will feel more like a minor inconvenience, paving the way to your beautifully extended home with fewer headaches and heartaches.

Keeping the Family Happy

Involving the Family in the Adventure

Transforming your house into a building site can seem daunting not just for you but for the entire family. However, this disruption doesn't have to be a strain. Instead, it can be an excellent opportunity for turning a potentially stressful experience into an exciting family adventure. The key here is involvement. When everyone's on board and active in the process, the sense of chaos subsides, replaced by a shared journey of creation.

Start by holding a family meeting to discuss the upcoming changes. Explain the timeline and what to expect in each phase of the extension project. Encourage questions and address any concerns openly. This meeting isn't just about passing information; it's about making everyone feel they have a stake in this family project.

You can assign roles suited to each family member's age and interest. Perhaps one of your children loves art? They could help design a colour scheme or choose wall art. Is there a budding engineer in the family? Involve them in understanding the architectural plans or the basics of the construction process. Even young children can pick out fixtures or give opinions on room layouts, making them feel part of the decision-making process.

Make it a point to regularly update each other on the progress. This could be through a weekly 'site meeting' over dinner, where each family member can express any thoughts or concerns and suggest ideas. These meetings ensure everyone feels heard and keeps the excitement alive, transforming the building site into a hive of family activity and anticipation.

Creating a Comfortable Environment with Reduced Space

While your home may resemble a construction zone, maintaining a semblance of normalcy is crucial for family happiness. The challenge of living in a reduced space doesn't mean you have to sacrifice comfort. It's all about optimising what you have.

Firstly, identify a space in your home that can remain untouched by the chaos. This could be a living room or a part of the house farthest from the construction. Make this your 'safe zone'—a place where the family can relax and unwind. Equip this area with comfortable seating, pleasant lighting, and favourite belongings. It's important this space feels like a retreat from the building activities.

Secondly, consider your temporary living arrangements. If the kitchen is being extended, set up a temporary kitchenette in another part of the house with essentials like a microwave, refrigerator, and kettle. This setup helps in maintaining some routine meal preparations and can be a fun camping-style adventure.

Storage solutions are also crucial in managing reduced living spaces. Use creative storage options to minimise clutter. Think vertically by using shelves, and consider multi-functional furniture like ottomans with storage or a couch that doubles as a guest bed. Keeping the space organised will help reduce stress and create a more livable environment despite the ongoing construction.

Celebrating Milestones

Every stage of your home extension project is a step closer to realising your dream home, and celebrating these milestones can greatly uplift the family spirit. Recognising progress, big or small, serves as a reminder of what you've achieved and what's soon to come.

You might celebrate when the foundations are laid, walls are built, or when windows are installed. Each of these phases is crucial and worth acknowledging. Plan small celebrations like a family pizza night, a movie evening, or a small outing. These don't have to be extravagant—simple acknowledgements are enough to boost morale and make the construction process enjoyable.

Another fun way to celebrate milestones could be through a visual timeline in your living space where you mark each completed stage of the project. Not only does this serve as a countdown to completion, but it also provides a visual representation of progress that the whole family can see and feel excited about.

You could even keep a photo diary or create a scrapbook of the construction phases. This not only documents the journey but can become a cherished keepsake, reminding your family of the adventure you shared and the collective effort that transformed your house into your dream home.

By involving your family in the adventure, creating a comfortable living environment, and celebrating milestones, the journey of extending your home can become a cherished memory rather than just a means to an end. Remember, the goal is to not just extend a house, but to build a dream and a stronger family bond along the way.

RECAP AND ACTION ITEMS

Surviving a home extension is no small feat, and you've just navigated through the essential strategies to make the process as smooth as possible. Let's quickly recap what you've learned and pinpoint some actionable steps to ensure you remain on top of things, even when your home looks more like a building site than a sanctuary.

Firstly, you've set the stage with thorough Planning Ahead, which is crucial. Ensure that you have a detailed timeline and budget that accounts for unexpected delays and expenses. This will not only save you from potential financial strain but will also keep stress levels at bay.

Action Step: Review your plan weekly, adjusting as necessary to stay on track.

You've also tackled Setting Up Temporary Spaces. Whether it's a makeshift kitchen or a cozy corner for relaxing, maintaining some normalcy is key.

Action Step: Keep these areas organised and tweak them to suit your daily needs, which will evolve as the project progresses.

On the topic of Builder's Storage, ensuring that tools and materials are stored safely and efficiently can drastically reduce hazards and inefficiencies.

Action Step: Regularly check that the agreed storage areas are being maintained properly to avoid any unnecessary disruptions.

Moving into Managing Stress and Disruption, maintaining your Routine During The Building Phase is vital. Whether it's sticking to regular meal times or your morning jog, keeping a routine can be incredibly grounding.

Action Step: Set small, attainable goals each week to maintain a sense of achievement.

Open Communication and Flexibility with your builders can significantly influence the project's smooth progression.

Action Step: Schedule weekly catch-ups with your contractor to discuss the progress and any adjustments needed.

Health and Safety cannot be overlooked. With all the chaos, ensuring that your living space is safe is crucial.

Action Step: Conduct bi-weekly safety checks around the house to identify and mitigate any potential risks.

Lastly, Keeping the Family Happy is paramount. Involving everyone in the family adventure can help turn the challenges into a shared journey.

Action Step: Hold a family meeting every fortnight to discuss how everyone is coping and make any needed adjustments to your living arrangements.

Creating a Comfortable Environment with reduced space involves smart organisation and perhaps even a bit of creativity.

Action Step: Reassess your temporary living spaces bi-weekly to ensure they still meet the family's needs.

And don't forget to Celebrate Milestones. Whether it's the completion of a critical phase or a particularly productive week, celebrating these moments can boost everyone's spirits.

Action Step: Plan small celebrations or rewards for these milestones to keep morale high.

By taking these steps, you can keep your life manageable and your family content, even amidst the dust and noise of building work. Remember, the chaos is temporary but the results will be your dream home. Stay focused, stay positive, and keep building towards your vision.

10

OVERCOMING COMMON PROBLEMS

"Expect the best, plan for the worst, and prepare to be surprised." - Denis Waitley

Budget Blowouts

Embarking on a home extension project is an exhilarating adventure, one that promises to morph your beloved abode into a more spacious and functional sanctuary. However, amidst the excitement, the looming threat of budget blowouts can dampen spirits and derail plans. Let's tackle this head-on, shall we? Understanding the potential pitfalls, strategising preemptively, and learning how to handle surprises will keep your project on track and your wallet intact.

Identifying Risk Factors

First things first, recognising what can cause your budget to swell is crucial. It's a bit like predicting the weather; you might not control it, but you can certainly prepare for it. One common risk factor is underestimating the scope of work. This might be due to over-optimistic planning or simply not accounting for the complexities involved in your specific project. It's easy to overlook elements like electrical upgrades or the need for site preparation based on soil quality.

Another significant risk is the 'unknown unknowns' – those hidden conditions or issues that only become apparent once the work begins. This could be anything from discovering damp that requires treatment, to realising that the existing building isn't up to code and needs additional work to bring it up to standard.

Changes in project scope, often initiated by you, the homeowner, can also lead to budget blowouts. It's common to start a project, then wish to add new features or use more premium materials than initially planned. While it's your prerogative to make changes, each alteration can inflate the budget significantly.

Lastly, not having a detailed contract or clear communication with your builder can leave room for budget blowouts. If the scope of work isn't clearly defined or is based on estimates rather than detailed quotes, unexpected costs can creep in.

Mitigation Strategies

Now, onto the defensive plays to keep those budget blowouts at bay. Start with precision planning. Before you even begin, invest time in defining every aspect of your project. This might mean consulting with architects, builders, and even interior designers to nail down a detailed plan and realistic budget.

Engage in thorough vetting of contractors. Don't just go with the first or cheapest option. Look for builders with stellar reputations and robust portfolios of completed projects. Check references and review past work to ensure they have a track record of staying on budget and on schedule.

Another key strategy is to insist on detailed, fixed-price contracts. These contracts should outline every aspect of the project, from timelines to materials and labour. The more detailed your contract, the less room there is for those pesky unexpected costs.

And what about those changes you might want to make mid-project? Implement a strict change order process. Any changes should require your approval, and you should understand how they will affect the overall budget. Sometimes seeing the cost implications on paper can help you decide whether a change is truly necessary.

Handling Unexpected Costs

Even with the best-laid plans, unexpected costs can and do arise. How you handle these can make the difference between a minor hiccup and a full-blown financial headache. First, it's wise to include a contingency fund in your budget from the outset. Industry standards suggest that this should be around 10-20% of the total project cost, depending on the complexity and scale of your extension.

When an unexpected cost does pop up, sit down with your contractor to fully understand the issue. Ask for it to be explained in detail, and discuss all possible solutions. Sometimes there's a more cost-effective option that you hadn't considered.

If the unexpected costs are substantial, it might be worth pausing the project momentarily to reassess your budget and funding options. This might mean securing additional financing or reevaluating the remaining project phases to see where costs can be trimmed.

Remember, keeping a cool head and maintaining open lines of communication with your builder and architect will help you navigate through the financial surprises that come your way.

In essence, managing a home extension project is as much about managing a budget as it is about design and construction. By identifying potential financial risks, setting up strategic barriers against overspending, and learning to adeptly handle surprises, you can steer your home extension to a successful and financially sound completion. Keep these pointers in mind, and you'll not only build an extension but also extend your prowess in savvy project management.

Planning Disputes

Resolving Conflicts with Authorities

When you're extending your home, getting into a tangle with local authorities over planning permissions can feel like a real setback. But fear not! These conflicts, while frustrating, can often be resolved with a good strategy and a bit of know-how.

First things first, make sure you fully understand why your application was rejected or why certain conditions were imposed. Often, the devil is in the detail. Local councils have comprehensive planning documents that can sometimes feel like they're written in another language. If you're struggling to decipher them, it might be worth consulting a planning consultant or an architect who specialises in local regulations. They can offer invaluable insights into the specific requirements of your local planning authority and help you see your plans from the council's perspective.

Once you've got to grips with the specifics, reach out to the planning officer assigned to your case. A direct conversation can clear up misunderstandings and provide a more personal approach to resolving issues. Be polite and professional, showing willingness to adapt your plans to meet regulations. You might be surprised at how flexible many planning officers are when they see you're trying to work with them rather than against them.

If minor modifications to your plans could lead to approval, consider making those changes. Sometimes, a few small tweaks here and there are all it takes to get the green light. Keep the communication channels open and document all interactions with the council, as this will help if you need to escalate the issue.

Legal Avenues

If dialogue and modifications don't sway the planning authorities, and you believe the decision to be unfair or legally flawed, it might be time to consider your legal options. Start with the appeals process. In the UK, you typically have the right to appeal a planning decision within a set period after receiving the decision notice, usually about three months.

The appeal process involves submitting a form to the Planning Inspectorate, and you can choose to have your appeal dealt with through written representations, a hearing, or an inquiry. The complexity of your case should guide your choice. For straightforward disputes, written representations are often sufficient. More complex issues, especially those involving legal intricacies or large-scale developments, might be better suited to a hearing or inquiry.

Prepare a robust case for your appeal. This is where having a planning consultant or solicitor can really pay off. They can help articulate the grounds of your appeal, ensuring that it is grounded in solid understanding of planning law and policy. Remember, the goal here is to demonstrate that the decision was not made in accordance with local planning policies, or that there were material considerations that were not properly taken into account.

Effective Negotiation Techniques

Negotiation is an art, especially when it comes to dealing with planning disputes. Effective negotiation can save you time, stress, and even money. The key is preparation and understanding both your position and that of the planning authority.

Before entering any negotiation, be clear about what you want to achieve and what you are willing to compromise on. Have a clear, ideally visual, presentation of your proposed changes and how they comply with or respect planning policies. This not only shows that you are professional and serious but also helps the planning officers visualise the end result.

Building a rapport with the planning officer can also make a significant difference. People are more likely to collaborate and find a middle ground if they feel respected and understood. Listen to their concerns and objections carefully, and address them systematically. Showing empathy towards their position and constraints can open up a dialogue that's more cooperative than confrontational.

Sometimes, bringing a third party into negotiations can help. Mediators or independent planning experts can provide a neutral perspective and often suggest creative solutions that might not have occurred to either party involved in the dispute.

Remember, the goal of negotiation is not to 'win' but to reach an agreement that allows your project to proceed while satisfying the regulatory requirements imposed by the planning authorities. Patience and persistence are your best allies here. Sometimes these discussions take time, and progress might seem slow, but with a balanced approach, you can navigate through these disputes effectively.

By addressing these common hurdles in planning disputes – from understanding the initial rejection and exploring legal avenues, to mastering the negotiations – you can steer your home extension project back on track. Each step offers a learning opportunity and a chance to refine your approach, ensuring that your dream home doesn't remain just a blueprint.

Construction Issues

Quality Issues

When you're extending your home, you want the finished product to mirror the glossy images in your head, right? However, one of the hiccups you may face along the journey involves quality issues. These could range from paint jobs that look like a child's first art project to fittings that come loose the first time you swing open a cabinet door. Here's how to keep a tight rein on quality.

Firstly, be meticulously clear about your expectations. When you communicate with your builder, clarity is your best friend. Use visuals, detailed descriptions, and samples to ensure there's no room for misinterpretation. Also, it's wise to have a detailed, written contract that includes the standards and materials to be used. This document can be your North Star if things start to go south.

Regular site visits are another crucial tactic. Don't be a stranger on your property; pop in unannounced if necessary. This shows the construction crew that you're keeping an eye on things, which in itself can be a massive incentive for them to maintain high standards.

If you do spot something off, address it immediately. Don't wait until the project is too far gone. Early intervention can prevent the snowball effect, saving you not just money but also future headaches.

Lastly, consider hiring an independent inspector or a quality assurance professional, especially for larger projects. Their expert eyes can catch what yours might miss, ensuring the work is up to the mark before it's too late.

Structural Problems

Now, let's talk about the backbone of your extension – its structure. Structural issues can range from minor annoyances to major safety hazards, so this isn't an area where you can afford to cut corners.

First off, always ensure you're working with certified and experienced professionals. When choosing a structural engineer, don't just go with the cheapest bid. Look into their background, check their credentials, and review past projects. It's like choosing a surgeon – you want the best hands you can afford. Structural engineers should ideally be Chartered Civil Engineer (MICE) or Chartered Structural Engineer (MIStructE) and carry Professional Indemnity Insurance to cover their work.

During the planning stage, invest in a thorough survey of your existing home and the site for the extension. This might seem like an unnecessary expense, but understanding the lay of the land and any potential challenges (like soil quality or underlying structures) can prevent monumental issues down the line.

If structural problems do arise during construction, it's crucial to hit pause on the project. This isn't the time for quick fixes. Consult with structural engineers and ensure the problem is fully analysed and understood before proceeding. Remedial actions may include reinforcing structures, altering designs, or even, in extreme scenarios, demolishing and rebuilding sections of the extension.

Document every step of dealing with structural issues. Don't rely on verbal advice, but get it in writing as either a report, letter, or email. Should anything go south in the future, having a detailed record is essential, especially if legal steps become necessary.

Remedial Actions

Encountering issues during the construction of your home extension isn't just common; it's almost expected. The key to moving forward is how effectively you handle these remedial actions.

First, establish a clear line of communication with your contractor about the remediation process. Define what needs to be fixed, how it should be fixed, and the timeframe for fixing it. This agreement should be in writing – consider this document as essential as any contract.

Sometimes, remedial actions might require bringing in specialists. For instance, if there's a significant issue with the electrical work, a certified electrician should be roped in rather than leaving it to general contractors. Yes, this can mean additional costs, but ensuring safety and quality in your home extension is non-negotiable.

Also, keep your local building control updated about any significant changes or remedial work being undertaken. They may need to re-inspect the work to ensure everything is up to code, providing you with the peace of mind that the corrections have indeed rectified the issues.

Lastly, learn from the snags. Once the dust has settled, review what went wrong and why. Was it a vetting issue with the contractors? Were there lapses in supervision? Understanding these can turn today's headaches into tomorrow's smooth sailing.

In navigating through these construction issues, remember that vigilance is your best defence. By staying informed, involved, and insistent on high standards, you'll steer your home extension project to success, avoiding the common pitfalls that snag many unwary homeowners.

RECAP AND ACTION ITEMS

By now, you've navigated through some of the trickiest terrains of home extension—budgeting, planning disputes, and construction hiccups. It's like you've been through a mini boot camp for homeowners. But what's the takeaway from all this? Let's boil it down to clear, actionable steps that you can implement to steer your home extension project to success, minimising stress and maximising satisfaction.

Firstly, let's talk money. You've learned the importance of identifying risk factors early on. This means keeping a keen eye out for anything that could inflate your costs down the line. Now, create a risk log. Include potential risks, their impact, and the probability of them occurring. Regularly review and update this document.

Next, develop a robust mitigation strategy. This could involve setting aside a contingency fund—typically 10-20% of your total budget—as a financial cushion for unexpected costs. Also, maintain open lines of communication with your contractors and suppliers to ensure there are no surprises.

When unexpected costs do hit, and they likely will, don't panic. Assess the situation calmly, consult your risk log, and use your contingency fund wisely. Remember, it's about damage control and keeping the project moving forward.

For planning disputes, remember, knowledge is power. Familiarise yourself with local building regulations and codes. This upfront investment of your time could save you from legal headaches later. If disputes arise, leverage the advice of a planning consultant early. Don't wait for small issues to become big problems.

Also, mastering effective negotiation techniques is crucial. Always approach disputes with a problem-solving mindset. Focus on interests rather than positions and look for win-win solutions. This will help maintain good relationships with all parties involved, which can be invaluable.

Lastly, for construction issues, vigilance is key. Regularly inspect the worksite and maintain a quality checklist. Your Building Control Officer is not there to inspect quality, so you will need to do this yourself or find someone else to do it on your behalf. If quality or structural issues arise, address them immediately with your contractor. Also, know your rights. If remedial work is needed, understand what warranties and guarantees cover your project to ensure these issues are resolved without additional cost to you.

Implementing these steps will require effort, persistence, and a proactive attitude. But remember, the goal is to build not just an extension, but a dream space for you and your family. Keep the end vision in mind, and let it motivate you through the challenges.

11

THE FINAL STRETCH: COMPLETION AND BEYOND

"Start by doing what's necessary; then do what's possible; and suddenly you are doing the impossible." - Francis of Assisi

Approaching the Finish Line

As you edge closer to the finish line of your home extension project, the excitement can be palpable. You're nearly there, about to reap the rewards of your careful planning and hard work. But before you can fully relax and enjoy your new space, there are a few crucial steps to ensure everything is up to scratch and officially complete. These are the final inspections, the creation of snagging lists, and obtaining the all-important completion certificates. Let's dive into each of these and make sure you cross that finish line with confidence and satisfaction.

Final Inspections

This is the moment of truth. Final inspections are not just a formality; they are your assurance that your extension meets all the required standards and regulations. Typically, your local council's building control will come in to carry out this inspection. They'll be checking to ensure all work completed matches up with the plans that were initially approved and that all building regulations have been adhered to.

During this inspection, it's essential to have your builder or contractor on hand. They can address any questions the inspector might have and make notes of any issues that need resolving. As a homeowner, your role here is to be as informed and involved as possible. Don't hesitate to ask questions. Understanding the specifics of what is being checked can give you peace of mind or prepare you for any potential issues that might arise.

Remember, this isn't just a bureaucratic hoop to jump through. Think of it as a protective measure – it's there to ensure that your home extension is safe, sound, and saleable. If the inspector finds issues, they will list what needs to be fixed before approval can be given. It's common, so don't let it dishearten you. See it as a step towards ensuring your extension is perfect.

Snagging Lists

Once the dust settles and the builders have packed away their tools, you might notice small issues or 'snags' that need addressing. These could range from a door that doesn't close properly to a missed painting spot on the ceiling. Creating a snagging list is your way of noting down all these minor faults or unfinished bits that you want to be rectified.

Walk through your new space with a critical eye, jot down anything that isn't up to the standard you expect. It's often helpful to do this with your contractor, as they can provide immediate feedback on what can be done and how quickly. This list then becomes the roadmap for the final touches on your project.

Snagging is a normal part of any construction project. It doesn't mean your builders have done a poor job. It's just the nature of building work that small things can be missed in the grand scheme of a larger project. Addressing these snags is crucial not only for the aesthetics and function of your extension but also for preventing minor issues from turning into major problems later on.

Obtaining Completion Certificates

Finally, obtaining your completion certificate from the building control body is the formal step that marks the end of the project. This certificate is crucial—it's proof that your extension complies with all the legal requirements and building regulations. Without it, you might face difficulties when you decide to sell your home, and it can even affect your home insurance.

Obtaining this certificate can take a bit of time, so factor this into your project timeline. Once all inspections are passed and any snags are fixed, your builder or architect will notify the local authority to issue the completion certificate. Keep this document safe; you will need it in the future.

Also, be aware that this isn't just about compliance. Your completion certificate is a testament to the safety and integrity of your new home space. It ensures that the work done meets the high standards required by law and provides you with peace of mind that your home extension is built to last.

In wrapping up, approaching the finish line of your home extension project is about ensuring that everything is as it should be, from compliance to comfort. The steps of final inspections, snagging, and obtaining completion certificates are your last hurdles. Handle these well, and you're set to move smoothly into your beautifully extended home, ready to start the next chapter of your life there.

Moving In

Preparation for Occupation

The moment has arrived: your dream extension is finally built, and it's almost time to step inside and start living in the newly crafted space. But before you cross the threshold, there's a critical phase of preparation that will ensure your transition into the new area is as seamless as possible. Think of this as setting the stage for the grand performance of everyday life in your expanded home.

Firstly, a thorough cleaning is paramount. Construction can leave behind a fine layer of dust and debris that you don't want to settle into your living spaces. Hiring professional cleaners who specialise in post-construction clean-up can make a big difference. They have the tools and know-how to deep clean nooks and crannies that regular cleaning might miss.

Next, consider the logistics of your utilities. Ensure that all services are fully operational—this includes checking that the plumbing, heating, and electrical systems are functioning correctly in the new parts of your home. It's a good idea to have a final walkthrough with your contractor to verify that everything is working as expected. This is also the perfect time to install or update your home security systems, including smoke detectors and carbon monoxide alarms, ensuring they cover the new extension.

Now, let's talk about the practical setup of your space. If your extension includes areas like kitchens or bathrooms, ensure all appliances are installed and ready to go. For living spaces, planning the layout of furniture and décor beforehand can alleviate a lot of stress. Use this as an opportunity to declutter and perhaps donate items you no longer need; there's no better time for a fresh start than when moving into a new part of your home.

Transitioning Smoothly

With preparation out of the way, the actual move into your new space should be an exciting, albeit busy, phase. Transitioning smoothly involves a few key strategies to integrate the new extension with the existing structure of your home.

First, continuity is key. Try to blend the old and new parts of the home in terms of design and functionality. If your extension feels like a separate entity, it could disrupt the flow of your living environment. Achieving a sense of continuity might involve minor adjustments or redecorations in your existing spaces to complement the extension.

Communication also plays a crucial role during this period. Keep regular contact with your contractor and any other professionals involved to address the inevitable minor issues that arise. Whether it's a last-minute paint touch-up or additional shelving that needs installing, keeping the lines of communication open will help resolve these issues promptly.

As you begin to use the new space, pay attention to how it feels and functions. Is the lighting adequate? Are there enough power outlets? Is the space as comfortable and practical as you envisioned? The first few weeks are a trial period where you can note what works and what might need tweaking.

Moreover, if the extension has introduced significant changes to your living environment, such as increased floor area or additional rooms, it might also change your daily routines. Allow yourself time to adjust to these changes. It might be rearranging your morning routine due to an additional bathroom or adapting to cooking meals in a larger kitchen. Embrace these changes gradually, allowing yourself and your family to naturally find your new rhythm in the enhanced home.

Immediate Aftercare

Once you're settled in, the focus should shift towards maintaining the beauty and functionality of your new extension. Immediate aftercare involves several crucial steps to ensure longevity and continued enjoyment of your investment.

Start with the basics: familiarise yourself with the care requirements of new materials and finishes. Whether it's the cleaning regimen for new countertops or the maintenance of newly installed floors, understanding how to properly care for these elements will keep them looking great for years to come.

Keep a vigilant eye on any signs of problems in the initial months. Issues like cracking, dampness, or unexpected settling should be addressed sooner rather than later to prevent bigger problems. Minor settlement and cracking should be expected to some extent, but this should settle down after the first few months. Having a third party warranty or snagging provision from your builder can be beneficial. Make sure you fully understand the terms and coverage so you can utilise it effectively if needed.

Regular maintenance checks are also essential. Create a schedule to inspect elements like seals, exteriors, and roofing periodically. This proactive approach will help catch and rectify minor issues before they escalate into major repairs, saving you time, stress, and money in the long run.

By focusing on these three areas—preparation, transition, and aftercare—you can ensure that moving into and living in your new home extension is as delightful and stress-free as possible. Remember, this is more than just an expansion of your physical space; it's an enhancement of your lifestyle, opening up new possibilities for you and your family. Embrace this new chapter with open arms and a well-prepared plan.

Post-Project Reflection

Evaluating Project Success

So, your dream extension is now a tangible reality. The dust has settled, and the sound of construction has faded into the background. It's time to reflect on the journey you've just completed. Evaluating the success of your project isn't just about admiring the new space (though that's certainly part of it); it's about understanding how the outcomes measure up against your initial goals.

Start by revisiting your original objectives. What were you aiming for? More kitchen space, an extra bedroom, or perhaps a sun-drenched conservatory? Align these goals with the end results. It's like checking off items on a grocery list – satisfying and surprisingly revealing. Did you achieve what you set out to do? If yes, take a moment to celebrate this success. If not, consider what factors might have led to these deviations.

Next, think about the budget. Staying on budget is often one of the most challenging aspects of home extensions. Did you manage to keep your finances in check? Overspending can be a common issue, but understanding where and why you overspent can provide valuable insights for future projects.

Maybe you opted for higher-quality materials or faced unforeseen structural challenges. Whatever the case, each of these decisions shapes the outcome and learning from them is crucial.

Quality is another critical factor. Assess the craftsmanship and finish of the work. Does everything look and function as expected? High-quality work not only satisfies aesthetically but also ensures durability. If there are areas that seem subpar, note these down for discussion with your contractor or for reference in future projects.

Finally, reflect on the timeline. Delays in construction projects can be frustrating and costly. Were there significant delays, and if so, what caused them? Sometimes delays are unavoidable, like those caused by weather or bespoke materials. Other times, they might be due to planning oversights or coordination mishaps. Understanding these can vastly improve the management of future home improvement ventures.

Lessons Learned

Every project, no matter how smoothly it goes, offers a treasure trove of lessons. These insights are invaluable; they refine your skills as a homeowner and make you more adept at handling future renovations or extensions.

One of the first areas to review is communication with your building team. Was there a clear line of communication established from the start? Effective communication can often be the make-or-break factor in the smooth running of a project. It ensures that your specifications are met and that any issues are swiftly addressed.

Consider the planning and design phase. Were there assumptions or oversights that led to changes mid-project? Sometimes what looks good on paper doesn't translate as well in real space. Learning from these instances can aid in better planning and design foresight in future projects.

Also, think about the stress factors. What parts of the project were most stressful, and why? Was it the disruptions to daily life, the financial investment, or decision fatigue from choosing fixtures and finishes? Identifying these stressors can help you develop strategies to mitigate them next time, perhaps by phasing the work differently, adjusting your budgeting approach, or delegating more decisions.

Lastly, consider the role of unexpected surprises. No matter how well you plan, unexpected challenges can arise—discovering an old piping system that needs replacing, for instance. Reflecting on how you and your team handled these surprises can be enlightening. Did you adapt quickly and effectively, or was it a scramble? This reflection can enhance your crisis management skills for any future renovations.

Planning for Future Projects

Now that you have one successful project under your belt, you might already be thinking about the next. Reflecting on what's just been completed not only prepares you for future projects but can also ignite excitement for new possibilities.

Begin by outlining what you would do differently based on your recent experience. Would you hire the same team? Use different materials? Change the scope? Documenting these points creates a ready checklist for future projects.

Consider also the aspects of the project that went particularly well. Maybe you found a fantastic electrician who worked efficiently and provided great advice, or you chose a floor material that has proven both beautiful and durable. Recognising these successes gives you a solid foundation to build upon next time.

If you're planning another project, think about the timing. Is there an ideal season or a particular life stage when the next round of renovations would fit best? Timing can significantly affect both the practicality and enjoyment of the project.

And finally, reflect on your readiness to jump into another project. Are you prepared for the disruption and investment again? Sometimes it's wise to pause and enjoy the fruits of your labour before diving back into the world of home improvement. Whatever your decision, this reflective process ensures that you're better equipped, more knowledgeable, and perhaps even a bit eager to tackle whatever project comes next.

Each of these reflective stages not only brings closure to your current project but also sets a strategic foundation for the future, ensuring that every home improvement experience is better than the last.

RECAP AND ACTION ITEMS

Congratulations! You are almost at the end of this life-changing journey. As you approach the final stages of your home extension project, you have navigated through the complexities of final inspections, snagging lists, and obtaining those all-important completion certificates. You're nearly ready to cross the finish line.

Firstly, give yourself a pat on the back. Handling the final inspections requires attention to detail and ensures that every aspect of the construction meets the required standards. Now, take a moment to review your snagging list. This is your tool to guarantee that every nook and cranny is exactly how you envisioned. Address these minor issues promptly with your contractor—it's your final push to perfect your dream space.

As you receive your completion certificates, store them safely. These documents are crucial for future reference, especially if you ever decide to sell your home.

Now, turn your attention to moving in. Start by preparing for occupation. This isn't just about moving boxes; it's about preparing your mind and your family for a new chapter in a renewed home. Plan the move-in day, thinking through logistics to ensure everything goes smoothly. As you transition, consider the immediate aftercare of your new space. Tend to the maintenance of new installations and understand the care they require.

Finally, take a deep breath and reflect on the completed project.

Evaluate the success against your initial goals. What worked well? What could have been better? Document these insights as they will be invaluable for any future projects. This reflective practice not only offers closure on this project but also sets a foundation for continuous improvement in any of your future endeavours.

Armed with these experiences, you're not just a homeowner; you're a savvy project overseer who's ready to tackle more, should you choose to. Whether it's another extension, a new building project, or simply enjoying the comfort of your upgraded home, remember that each step you take builds more than just physical spaces—it builds dreams.

ACTION STEPS:

1. Finalise the snagging list with your contractor and confirm completion
2. Safely store all relevant documents, including completion certificates
3. Plan and execute your moving day, considering the needs of your family and the specifics of the new space
4. Schedule a day within a month after moving in to reassess the space and address any emerging concerns
5. Set aside an evening to jot down the successes and lessons learned from this project, using these notes as a blueprint for future projects or adjustments.

By following these steps, you ensure that the completion of your home extension is just the beginning of a new, exciting phase in your life. Enjoy every moment in your newly expanded home, filled with memories yet to be created.

SEIZE YOUR FUTURE: A CALL TO ACTION

As you close the final pages of this journey, it is paramount to reflect not just on the practical steps and strategies discussed but on the expansive horizon that now lies before you. The path has been charted through meticulous planning, innovative designs, and an understanding of the legal frameworks that scaffold your ventures. Now, the real adventure begins.

The essence of this book is not merely to inform but to transform; it is about envisaging a future that beckons with limitless possibilities and seizing it with both hands. You have been equipped with the tools, insights, and methodologies that are the hallmarks of successful projects across the globe. What remains is for you to step out and put these into practice.

Visionaries like you are rare — individuals who dream big but are also prepared to lay the groundwork to manifest those dreams into reality. Remember, the world we live in was built by people who dared to look beyond the status quo and challenge the confines of the existing. Now, more than ever, the world needs innovators who are not just thinkers but doers.

However, even the most seasoned pioneers know that the

journey towards realising monumental projects is seldom a solitary trek. Collaboration, advice, and ongoing support from seasoned professionals can illuminate parts of the path that may otherwise be fraught with uncertainties. Whether it's navigating new regulatory environments or overcoming unforeseen challenges, having a guide can make all the difference.

So, as you stand on the precipice of what could be the most thrilling chapter of your professional life, consider this: the support you need to elevate your project from concept to completion is just a connection away. If you find yourself seeking guidance or needing expert advice tailored to your unique circumstances, do not hesitate to reach out.

Imagine a partnership where your visionary ideas are met with cutting-edge solutions and strategic insights that only years of dedicated experience can provide. By connecting, you're not just accessing services, you're engaging a dynamic ally dedicated to ensuring your vision not only sees the light of day but flourishes in the fullness of its potential.

As you move forward, let each step be bold and intentional. The world awaits the imprint of your innovation, and every moment is an opportunity to craft a legacy that resonates across time. Your journey has been enriched with knowledge and strategies, but it is your actions that will define the future.

Consider this not as an end but as an invitation to begin something extraordinary. The tools and understanding you have acquired are the foundation. How high and how far you build upon them will be your legacy. Do not shy away from reaching out if doing so can bring your dreams closer to reality. In collaboration, there is strength, and in partnership, there is potential magnified beyond what one can achieve alone.

If you feel ready to take that step, to not just dream but to actualise your dreams, visit www.robindejongh.com. Here, you can connect with a team that understands your vision, shares your passion, and is committed to helping you succeed. Together, let us build not just structures, but a future that inspires.

Every chapter in this book has been an invitation to challenge the conventional, to embrace the innovative and to understand the profound impact thoughtful design and execution can have on the world. As you turn each page, remember that knowledge is not just for contemplation but for action.

The blueprint for success has been laid out; the strategies and insights, shared. Now, the pen is in your hand, and the blank pages of your venture await your script. Dream big, plan meticulously, and act courageously. The world is not just a stage but a canvas, and you are the artist.

Remember, every great achievement begins with the decision to try. Trust your vision, engage with the best, and transform your aspirations into reality. Visit www.robindejongh.com today, and let's make your vision come to life.

This is your time for Building Dreams.

About the Contributors

Robin de Jongh

Robin de Jongh is a highly respected Chartered Civil Engineer with an illustrious career spanning over three decades in the construction industry. A member of the Institution of Civil Engineers, Robin was a global finalist in the Institution's Emerging Engineers Award, reflecting his innovative approach and commitment to engineering excellence.

Robin is the author of several books for Packt Publishing and Woodland Press. Beyond his written contributions, Robin is a dynamic speaker who has delivered presentations at prestigious events such as TEDx and Ecobuild. His insightful articles have been featured in leading technology magazines, sharing his extensive knowledge and experience with a wide audience.

Robin is best know for his popular YouTube channel, where he provides valuable content for homeowners, builders, and industry professionals. His channel features comprehensive tutorials, product reviews, and expert advice, empowering viewers with the information they need to tackle their construction projects confidently.

Robin runs Woodland Consulting, a structural engineering consultancy in the Midlands, England. www.woodland.consulting

Geraint Davies - Technical Reviewer

Geraint Davies brings over 30 years of experience in building construction and property development, encompassing roles such as carpenter & joiner, property developer, site manager/foreman, building clerk of works, and currently a building control officer for a local authority. He holds a BSc (Hons) in Building Maintenance, Surveying, and Management, alongside an HNC and ONC in Construction. Geraint is also certified with a National Award in Construction and an NVQ Level 2 in Carpentry & Joinery.

His qualifications include advanced training in site management safety (SMSTS), emergency first aid at work (EFAW), and IOSH Managing Safety. Geraint has extensive experience ensuring compliance with building regulations for extensions and new builds. His breadth of knowledge and hands-on expertise made him a vital contributor to the book, providing valuable insights and quality assurance.

Milan Mathew George - Technical Reviewer

Milan Mathew George holds a Master of Engineering in Construction Engineering and Management and brings over 16 years of extensive experience in the engineering industry. His career spans across multiple countries, including Canada, India,

Oman, and the UAE, where he has served in various capacities such as Director, CEO, Project Manager, Technical Manager, and Senior Structural Engineer.

Milan is a practicing Professional Engineer (P.Eng.) in Canada since 2022 and has been a certified Project Management Professional (PMP) since 2019. He is also a Certified Provisional Lead Auditor of the Chartered Quality Institute (CQI) and an Indian Municipal Licensed Engineer-A since 2010. His diverse expertise covers a wide range of sectors including oil and gas, residential and commercial buildings, infrastructure, and service utilities.

Allan Cunningham - Technical Reviewer

Allan Cunningham is a seasoned Civil Engineer and Building Surveyor with extensive experience in the construction and engineering industries. He holds professional registrations with the Board of Engineering (BOETT) and the Institute of Surveyors of Trinidad and Tobago (MISTT). Allan's career spans over several decades, during which he has prepared architectural, structural, and MEP drawings, and progressed through roles as a civil engineer, building surveyor, project manager, and quality manager for contractors.

Allan's expertise includes managing the development of housing units, adaptive conversion projects, and providing forensic and condition reports for buildings and infrastructure. He has taught engineering surveying, drafting, construction practice, and project management to technicians and professionals, enhancing their technical and administrative skills. His experience extends to managing large teams, overseeing public sector change processes, and participating in high-value construction projects, including healthcare facilities, educational institutions, and commercial developments.

Russ Oakes - Technical Reviewer

Russ Oakes is an experienced professional in architecture, design, and engineering, specializing in planning consultancy since 2009. He is a Registered Electrical Engineer (NAPIT), a Registered Gas Engineer (Gas-Safe), and a Registered Member of the Institute of Engineering & Technology (TMIET). With a comprehensive background in architectural design and structural engineering, Russ has been involved in both domestic and small commercial projects, offering full project management services.

He has collaborated with various trades to ensure projects are completed on time and within budget. His expertise includes domestic extensions, full builds, small commercial extensions, and some industrial project planning.

Also by Robin de Jongh

How to Become a Self Employed Civil or Structural Engineer
How to Break Free and Thrive as a Self-employed Civil or Structural Engineer.

Imagine spending years studying and working hard to become a civil or structural engineer, only to find yourself stuck in the rut of a 9-to-5 job, dreaming of independence but terrified of taking that leap. It's hardly your fault. In today's complex business environment, the security of a steady paycheck is comforting, but it also holds many back from reaching their full potential.

This is where this book comes in. Crafted for engineers like you, it guides you step-by-step from the initial setup of your consultancy through to expanding your business successfully.

Printed in Great Britain
by Amazon